A Biblical Guide To Understanding
Impairments, Afflictions, & Suffering
Within Today's World

BARRIERS
AND
BRIDGES

by

GEORGE BURGESS

Aadeon Publishing Company
Hartford

All rights reserved. No part of this book may be reproduced in
any form without permission in writing from the publisher,
except in the case of brief quotations embodied in critical
articles or reviews.

All scripture quotations, unless otherwise indicated, are taken from the
New King James Version®. Copyright © 1982 by Thomas Nelson, Inc.
Used by permission. All rights reserved.

Scripture designated NIV is from the New International Version®.
Copyright © 1973, 1978, 1984 by International Bible Society.
Used by permission of Zondervan Publishing House.
All rights reserved.

Scripture designated KJV is from the King James Version.

Barriers and Bridges: A Biblical Guide To Understanding,
Impairments, Afflictions, & Suffering Within Today's World

Copyright © 2005
George Burgess

Published by Aadeon Publishing Company
P.O. Box 223
Hartford, CT 06141

Library of Congress Catalog Number: 2004094369
International Standard Book Number 0-9759070-0-X

Printed in the United States of America

Contents

Introduction	5
Chapter 1 Identity Lost	7
Chapter 2 Who Sinned	22
Chapter 3 The Thorn	35
Chapter 4 The Burdens	50
Chapter 5 The Agony of Victory	64
Chapter 6 The Calling	74
Chapter 7 The Comforter's Care	87
Chapter 8 The Fellowship Factor	99
Chapter 9 Facing Frustration, Bitterness, and Rejection	122
Chapter 10 A Tribute to the Triumphant	135
Small Group Study Questions	143
Helpful Organizations and Agencies	153
Scripture Index	156
Subject Index	160

Introduction

All people at some point in their lives will encounter impairments, afflictions, and suffering—either personally or in the lives of friends and family. Such things have been with us from the earliest days of man and will continue.

Given the nature of the problems we will encounter, it is essential each of us know what the Bible says about this important area of life. Waiting for the moment we or someone we care about encounters such things is the wrong time to learn about them. When faced with times of trouble, when knowledge and strength are necessary, we must be prepared to weather the storm and help others as well.

The pages of this book are dedicated to helping all people better understand the issues, concerns, and wisdom offered through the Bible on this subject.

It is important to note that striving to be sensitive to everyone reading this book is a primary goal of the author. As a result, you will notice terms such as impaired, afflicted, and suffering being used often. These terms are used frequently to avoid using others considered offensive by some people.

This is one of the most important subjects you can read about and share with others. I encourage you to carefully read the book, and share word of it with others. Education is the best way to prepare for times of trouble. Be ready. Be prepared. Help others do likewise!

Dedication

This book is dedicated to those
who struggle daily with impairments,
afflictions and suffering.

Acknowledgment

I would like to thank Carol
for the role she played in
the development of this book.

1 Identity Lost

One arm, one leg, and a single eye? War can be a very trying time for parents. Many live from letter to letter, hoping and praying their soldier, airman, or seaman will survive another day of battle. Such was the case for one couple who had not heard from their son for several months. No letters, phone calls or news caused them to believe the seaman had died in battle.

Then one day the phone rang out and to their amazement their son was on the line. As they spoke, he told them he had failed to write because he had been caring for a fellow sailor who had been injured. He spoke of how the young man had lost an arm, a leg, and an eye as his parents listened with much concern. In time the young man mustered the courage to ask his parents if his friend could come and live with them. He noted the sailor did not have another home to go to.

After some discussion, the seaman's parents told him they felt the burden of caring for such a badly wounded person would be too much for them. As the conversation closed, the seaman expressed his love and told his parents he understood their concerns. The following morning the couple received a telegram from naval authorities informing them their son had died. The message stated that he had jumped from a window to his death.

The message stunned the parents. They could not understand why their son had reacted as he did. But when the casket arrived and was opened, their son's lifeless body spoke volumes. There he lay, with only one arm, one leg, and a single eye.[1]

The Person

The physically impaired—who are they? They are our sons and daughters, our mothers and fathers, our sisters and brothers. They're our grocers, repairmen, teachers, and mayors. Like most people, including the Lord Jesus Himself, each of us at some point in our lives is likely to experience some sort of physical impairment. Whether at birth, during middle age, or in the golden years, impairments are almost inevitable.

As certain as such things are, when we are young and healthy we may fail to empathize with the struggles of the afflicted. For many of us, the physically impaired are less than a passing thought. Of course when we see the impaired, we feel bad for them. We may even stop to politely open a door or two. But beyond that, for most of us the impaired tend to be "out of sight, out of mind."

In fairness, we need not be cruel, cold-hearted people to display this mentality. All of us by nature tend to focus only on those things that are most relevant to us. Even if something is very relevant, our ability to relate to a foreign experience is limited.

Over the years, I have ministered to many who were physically impaired. I have visited people in poorly run state nursing homes, exclusive retirement estates, hospitals and private homes. This might lead some to believe I am better equipped to relate to the many difficulties the impaired regularly experience. This is not the case. Apart from experiencing such a thing, it is difficult to appreciate the trials they encounter daily. Even those who spend large sums of time with the impaired find it difficult to obtain a deep understanding of their plight.

---

1. Donald E. Wildmon, "Their Son Came Home," Tupelo, MS *American Family Association*, (June, 1994): 1.

How do people who are not impaired relate with the endless darkness of the blind, the loss of movement of the lame, the still quietness of the deaf, the weakness of the terminally ill? We cannot relate with their trials. I came to realize this the hard way.

For most of my life I was the picture of health and fitness. I was an accomplished athlete and a member of the elite US Army Rangers. The physical standards and demands set by the Rangers were among the highest in the military. For me, all of this changed one afternoon while inspecting a tree stand. One moment I was securely in a tree, and before I knew it, I lost my balance. I decided to jump to the safety of the moist ground. Unfortunately, instead of hitting the spongy surface, my right foot landed squarely on a large bulging root.

After X-rays had been taken, my surgeon told me I had broken my heel in four places and shattered the joint as well. He said it was one of the most serious breaks a person could incur. To my dismay, in the span of twenty-four short hours, I went from being a healthy, mobile person to someone who would be physically impaired for the rest of his life.

When I contemplated the depth of my injury, I was sickened at the thought. The idea of metal pins and a plate holding the shattered pieces of my foot together was heart breaking. Graciously the Lord did not allow me to dwell on this for long. He reminded me that the outcome could have been much worse. This led me to view my impairment not as a curse, but as an aid to help me better relate with a special group of people.

As a result of the Lord's encouragement, I felt moved to learn about the world of the physically impaired, rather than run from it. As I did, I realized there is a segment of people who regularly face trials I could never have imagined. I began to learn that things most of us take for granted—showers, putting on a pair of pants, using the stairs, etc.—can be major obstacles for some people. Something as basic as turning over while sleeping can be a source of extreme fear and terrible pain.

Through my experience, I came to realize we must strive to be much more sensitive to the plight of the physically impaired. Many of them badly need our help and encouragement; not because they are weak or inferior, but like all of us, they need the support of others.

The physical loss and emotional trials they face daily can weigh heavily on them. We cannot fully understand their difficulties, but we can certainly try. We must avoid morbidly dwelling on such things, while being as sensitive as possible to their ongoing struggles.

Regardless of man's ability or inability to empathize with the physically impaired, we know the Lord Jesus truly loves them. He proved this during His earthly ministry. Countless times He was found ministering to the physically impaired. Over and over again He was seen healing their feeble bodies. He paid some of them the highest honor by recording their personal stories in the Bible.

If Christ loved the physically impaired so much that He spent time with them, healed them, included them in His Word, and even died for them, then we too must recognize their importance and act accordingly.

Their Plight

The physically impaired are a very special group of people. They are special because they are loved by the Lord and because they have contributed a great deal to humanity. Beethoven overcame his inability to hear sounds to compose some of the greatest symphonies ever performed. Roosevelt could not stand unassisted, yet proudly served three terms as president of the United States. In the world of sports, pitcher Jim Abbot, born with one arm, pitched a no-hit baseball game while playing for the legendary New York Yankees.

The physically impaired have also contributed academically, vocationally, and culturally to the furtherance of society. Many have strengthened our nation by endeavoring to raise healthy families and act as models of moral excellence.

Like any other person, they face the trials of everyday life and much, much more. Some regularly struggle through the pain of physical therapy—muscles, bones, joints and tendons being exorcized like demons. Others valiantly make their way through the darkness of day from one location to the next.

Their example of personal courage and determination has inspired others to become more resourceful and productive people. The world as a whole has been enriched by their presence and contributions.

Even with such accolades, there are those who do not appreciate their presence or their plight. To some, they are burdens on society. To others, they should never have been born. In an article titled, "The Handicapped Are Normal People," Harrison F. Parsons Jr. wrote:

DEAR ABBY:

> I was born with German measles, which left me deaf, blind in one eye and 50 percent brain damaged, but I feel fortunate to be alive. All my life I have tried to get people to be a little more patient with handicapped people, because I have been discriminated against because of my disabilities, and I hate discrimination.
>
> I wrote a piece for my 12th grade high school public-speaking class presentation. It was *'The Handicap Plea.'* I am sending you a copy, hoping you will print it and wake up some people to realize that handicapped people are normal.
>
> **The Handicap Plea**
>
> We the handicapped may look strange. But look around carefully, we all have the same needs. As nature goes, we all have the same form of body. But some part of our body may be missing or deformed. Some parts of us may not function the same way as yours do. We may lose it at birth, or get hurt in an accident or have a disease. But we are lucky to be alive and are willing to sacrifice for that.
>
> Normal people can become handicapped from old age, accident, war or disease. If you look around carefully, you will understand that people who are handicapped are just like people who are not. We are still people, who want the chance to walk the golden road to success. We don't ask you to give us success, just the chance to succeed without put-downs or ridicule. You can give us the courage to succeed.

> You look at nature as a thing of beauty, yet no two snowflakes are alike. We would be honored to be treated the same, because we know your needs are the same as ours. The needs we all have are physical (natural), emotional and spiritual. So after all is said and done, please give us the chance and encouragement to prove to all that people who are handicapped are normal people![2]

Why is it people like Harrison must endure put-downs, ridicule, discouragement and a sense of abnormality? The reasons are many, but two stand out above the rest. Chuck Colson touched upon one reason when he said:

> If you ever visit Auschwitz, it's one of the most bone-chilling experiences you'll ever have. You'll see a huge sign at the entrance with Adolf Hitler's words: 'I want to raise a generation devoid of conscience.' Isn't it ironic that Hitler, a madman, attempted to raise a generation devoid of conscience, but he failed because the civilized world rose up and fought him? Yet here in America, through our indolence and our apathy, we are doing exactly what Hitler tried to do. The only difference is that we are doing it unconsciously.[3]

Unconsciously we are raising generations devoid of conscience, because for years we have consciously abandoned biblical principles of right and wrong. What keeps a society from ridiculing the physically impaired? An ethically sound and biblically sensitive conscience, built on a system of moral absolutes. Apart from this, the physically impaired, as well as unwanted, unborn children, the elderly, and in some cases the terminally ill, will continue to suffer the merciless darts of man's depravity.

The weak, the helpless and the innocent have increasingly suffered needless ridicule due to a regressive change in attitude. This change has worked to erode the basic worth of human life.

---

2. Harrison F. Parsons Jr., "The Handicapped Are Normal People," Dear Abby, (August 19, 1986).
3. Chuck Colson, "Where Did Our Conscience Go?," *Focus On The Family*, (January 1994): 14.

This is affirmed in a statistical abstract from the US Bureau of the Census in 1989. The abstract indicates that between the years 1950 and 1988, suicide increased 100 percent, abortion increased 800 percent, and euthanized patients increased 1,200 percent.

Clearly, these examples bear witness to a drastic change in society's view of life—mothers killing their unborn children, individuals taking their own lives, doctors encouraging euthanasia and medicide. How is this possible? It begins with our perception of man, his worth, his uniqueness, and especially his origin.

Simply put, the way we view man tends to dictate the way we treat men in general. If our understanding of man and his relevance is high, then we are prone to value him greatly. If our opinion is low, there is an increased possibility we will devalue his essential worth.

Their Image

One day, while watching a sporting event on television, a commercial advertising a well-known product appeared. The theme of the advertisement was "Image Is Everything." Repeatedly, the spokesman encouraged the viewer to consider the tremendous importance of the "right" image.

The advertiser was correct when asserting that "Image Is Everything." The way we perceive something tends to dictate the way we relate to it. Again, the physically impaired (and man in general) have been undergoing an image change for some time now. The change has slowly impacted the way we view and even treat others. Today, two major schools of thought direct the way we view people. One school perceives humans as magnificent mammals; the other as magnificent men. On the surface the difference may seem minimal, but as we shall see, one view degrades man while the other rightly exalts him.

Magnificent Mammal?

Since the days of Charles R. Darwin and his book *The Origin of Species*, there has been an increasing emphasis on man—the magnificent mammal. The heart and soul of such thinking is based on the theory of evolution. In short, the theory holds that all life found its beginning through the generation of a single living cell. It is believed the cell developed from a simple to a highly complex form of life over the course of billions of years.

As a product of evolution, theorists have classified man as a mammal. A mammal, no matter how magnificent, is nothing more than an animal. Those who promote this theory believe man and animal to be the same species. In other words, they are related.

This teaching has been wonderful news for the animal kingdom. As man's "relative," their worth and rank has been elevated closer to man's. On the other hand, the theory has worked to decrease the value of humans by lowering them to the status of the "supreme" animal.

As assertive as evolutionists have been in this regard, others note the theory's lack of credible support. Jack W. Sears, in his book *Conflict and Harmony in Science and the Bible,* says:

> The evidence for human evolution is fragmentary and fraught with difficulties of interpretation. The picture is far from clear that the human species has evolved at all.[4]

Paul D. Ackerman, in his book *It's a Young World After All,* adds:

> Evolutionists around the world have had to learn the hard way that evolution cannot stand up against creationism in any fair and impartial debate situation where the stakes are the hearts and minds of intelligent, undecided—but nevertheless objective and open-minded-audiences.[5]

In *The Collapse of Evolution* Scott M. Huse establishes the mathematical impossibility of evolution:

> Modern research by NASA has demonstrated that the most basic type of protein molecule that could be classified living is

---

4. Jack W. Sears, *Conflict and Harmony in Science and the Bible* (Grand Rapids: Baker Book House, 1969) p. 71.
5. Paul D. Ackerman, *It's a Young World After All* (Grand Rapids: Baker Book House, 1986) p. 13.

composed of at least 400 linked amino acids. Each amino acid, in turn, is made up of a specific arrangement of four or five chemical elements, and each chemical element is itself a unique combination of protons, neutrons, and electrons![2] Golay has demonstrated that the chance formation of even the simplest replicating protein molecule is 1 in 10^{450}.[3] Wysong has calculated the probability of forming the proteins and DNA for the smallest self-replicating entity to be 1 in $10^{167,626}$, even when granting astronomically generous amounts of time and reagents![4] Who can imagine what the chance formation of a more complex structure or organ such as the cerebral cortex in the human brain would be? It contains over 10,000,000,000 cells each of which is carefully arranged according to a specific design, and each of which is fantastically complex in itself . . . Given the exceedingly small probabilities of the preceding discussion (e.g. 1 in 10^{375}, 1 in 10^{450}, 1 in $10^{1,000}$, and 1 in $10^{167,626}$), it is very significant to note that mathematicians generally consider any event with a probability of less than one chance in 10^{50} as having a zero probability, i.e., it is impossible.[6]

Given the observations of people like Sears and Ackerman, coupled with the overwhelming mathematical impossibilities noted by Huse, how does one explain the wide support of the theory within the scientific community? Dr. Robert Jastrow, astronomer, author, and self-proclaimed agnostic, sheds light on the rudiments of the secular scientist's mind-set, saying:

> Scientists cannot bear the thought of a natural phenomenon which cannot be explained, even with unlimited time and money. There is a kind of religion in science; it is the religion of a person who believes there is order and harmony in the Universe. Every event can be explained in a rational way as the product of some previous event; every effect must have its cause; there is no First Cause.[7]

---

6. Scott M. Huse, *The Collapse of Evolution* (Grand Rapids: Baker Book House, 1986) p. 88-89.

Dr. Jastrow goes on to add:

> This religious faith of the scientist is violated by the discovery that the world had a beginning under conditions in which the known laws of physics are not valid, and as a product of forces or circumstances we cannot discover. When that happens, the scientist has lost control. If he really examined the implications, he would be traumatized. As usual when faced with trauma, the mind reacts by ignoring the implications.[8]

Here we see an impartial acknowledgement that the scientific mind, apart from any evidence, tends to be biased against "natural phenomenon which cannot be explained." Thus, there appears to be a strong predisposition within some, if not most, that encourages them to automatically bypass such things as creationism in favor of evolutionism. Why? Because one jibes with their hidden predisposition whereas the other does not.

This leads us to believe that in matters such as the origin of the universe and the "birth" of man, the credibility and objectivity of some scientists is questionable. Therefore, when seeking to develop a realistic image of man, we must be mindful of the fact that many of the proponents of the magnificent mammal concept are extremely partial in their views. We must also refrain from viewing evolution as a fact, maintaining an ironclad exterior. Clearly, it is far from being a fact and is void of any real certainty.

Magnificent Man!

When you look in the mirror, what do you see? Do you see the remnants of a highly evolved ape or something much greater?

In the Bible, the book of Genesis provides a very different view of man's origin from that of the evolutionary theory. Genesis chapter 1 verses 26 through 27 says:

---

7. Robert Jastrow, *God And The Astronomers* (New York: Warner Books) p. 123. Some consider Dr. Jastrow to be one of the leading astronomers of all times.
8. Ibid., p. 123.

Then God said, "Let Us make man in Our image, according to Our likeness; let them have dominion over the fish of the sea, over the birds of the air, and over the cattle, over all the earth and over every creeping thing that creeps on the earth." So God created man in His own image; in the image of God He created him; male and female He created them.

Genesis 2:7 details the origin of man, saying, "The Lord God formed man of the dust of the ground, and breathed into his nostrils the breath of life; and man became a living being."

Verses 21 through 22 conclude the account by describing the creation of the female creature, saying:

> And the Lord God caused a deep sleep to fall on Adam, and he slept; and He took one of his ribs, and closed up the flesh in its place. Then the rib which the Lord God had taken from man He made into a woman, and He brought her to the man.

As we skim through these verses, several things stand out. At first glance, we see the Bible portrays man as a creature. God created man. Thus, from a biblical perspective, man did not evolve. The craftsman was not chance, but God Himself. He personally formed man and "breathed" the "breath of life" into him.

Secondly, we see man was distinct in many ways from animals. Man was created apart from animals. Man was given rule over all the animals of the earth. God Himself named man, while allowing man to name the animals. Man was given a will to make moral decisions—animals were not. Man communicated with God and was aware of His supremacy. Clearly, Scripture portrays man not as one of the animals, but completely distinct from them.

The third thing that stands out is that God created man "in His own image." From a biblical standpoint, this is a very important factor in determining the overall worth of mankind. If man was truly created in God's image, he could not have evolved from animals. If this is true, we are compelled to view man's life more highly than that of an animal. Consequently, we are held to a higher standard of accountability for the way we treat men. Biblically speaking, respect for humanity equates respect for God, His image, and even His sovereignty.

Dignity and Worth

What is the fundamental difference between evolutionism and creationism? Between a magnificent mammal and a magnificent man? The ability to truly comprehend man's essential dignity and worth. Touching upon this, Francis A. Schaeffer said:

> Once one removes the createdness of all things, meaning and categories can only be some sort of leap, with or without drugs, into an irrational world. Modern man's blackness, therefore, rests primarily upon his losing the reality of the createdness of all things.[9]

Without God, man's dignity and worth are no longer determined by a supreme authority, but by the world he lives in. To whatever extent human reason grants worth, man has worth, and to whatever extent human reason denies worth, man lacks worth.

Without a supreme authority setting absolute moral standards, there is no reason to treat the physically impaired, nor anyone else, with dignity and respect. If the impaired are not created in God's image, they are nothing more than magnificent mammals gone bad! They are glitches on the screen of life—a flaw in the evolutionary process that will one day be eradicated.

In this new age, what do the physically impaired lack? Dignity! In an article titled "Accept the Disabled," Robert A. Bernstein spoke of Elizabeth Bouvia, a twenty-year-old Californian with cerebral palsy. At the time of the article, Ms. Bouvia was actively seeking the approval of the California State Supreme Court to help her end her life.

Mr. Bernstein noted Ms. Bouvia had reached this point because of the high level of societal bias toward the physically impaired. To support her feelings, Bernstein pointed out that "The Federal Rehabilitation Act of 1973 specifically recognized social prejudices as the cause of our failure to integrate the disabled" into society.[10]

---

9. Francis A. Schaeffer, *Genesis in space and time* (Downers Grove: InterVarsity Press, 1972) p. 32.

In a similar article in *The New York Times*, Gina Kolata said:

> When the disabled choose death, advocates say, they are demonstrating that society has made life so difficult that it may seem not worth living. 'The difficulty is not in being disabled,' said Mary Johnson, editor of *The Disability Rag* . . . ' It's in the way we treat disabled people.[11]

How would some like to treat the physically impaired? An article in *The Wall Street Journal* titled "Can't We Put My Mother to Sleep?" gives us a clue. Here the author links the life of his ninety-year-old mother to that of his boyhood dog, Jerry. Mom, like Jerry, is old and impaired, and the writer feels that mom, like the dog, should be humanely "put to sleep."[12]

Do you notice the unusual link? The physically impaired long for death because of society's poor treatment of them. Imagine, a son looking to put his mother to sleep like the family dog!

A New Reality

The evolutionary theory leads us to view humans not as unique creatures created in God's image, but as animals. Is it any wonder society's perception of man has changed so drastically? Is it any wonder abortion, euthanasia, medicide, and suicide have increased so dramatically? For many, evolutionary principles have replaced biblical ones. The harvest of this wicked seed is the slow deterioration of man's dignity and worth.

How is this possible? Over time people have begun to slowly accept a new form of reality. Within it God is no longer supreme—man is. The Bible is not the ultimate moral guide—opinion and consensus are. Acknowledging this ever-increasing

---

10. Robert A. Bernstein, "Accept The Disabled," *The New York Times*, (January 10, 1984): 23.
11. Gina Kolata, "Saying Life Is Not Enough, The Disabled Demand Rights And Choices," *The New York Times*, (January 31, 1991): B7.
12. Alan L. Otten, "Can't We Put My Mother to Sleep?," *The Wall Street Journal*, (June 5, 1985).

change is important because our perception of reality is man's mental and moral starting point. What we are and what we shall be are conditioned by the way we view reality. Unquestionably, those who see reality through a biblical framework will view some important issues differently from those who perceive it from a non-biblical perspective.

To some this new reality is a giant leap forward. It is seen as breaking away from the ancient shackles of a religious mind-set. But as we have seen, while such people break away from one form of religion, they replace it with another.

The change and the battle that accompany it is real. The prize is nothing less than the hearts and minds of future generations and the society they live in. Signs of this new reality permeate the landscape. That which was once considered immoral is viewed as "progressive" and "cutting edge." Morality from a black-and-white perspective is a thing of the past. Gray is the color of the day.

Knowingly or unknowingly the new reality has encouraged the disintegration of such cherished virtues as biblically defined love, family, order, justice, morality and even the value of life. And as we have seen, it has had a profound effect on the physically impaired and how some in society view them.

Beyond the issue of dignity and worth lies a much greater question. Where will this new reality lead us? Today's pundits demand "choice." They say it's a person's right to choose to abort, commit suicide or medicide. "Quality of life" is the noble hook here. Yet if this sort of thinking prevails, the severely impaired are merely one step closer to the next extreme.

Once "freedom of choice" becomes the standard, the choice may one day evolve into an obligation. An obligation to escape the bondage of suffering, to free family, friends, and society of the medical, emotional, and financial burdens associated with severe impairments. Today we may have a hard time imagining such a terrible thing occurring, but if conditions such as extreme overcrowding and shortages of resources begin threatening the welfare of society, it could happen. With foundational principles such as Darwin's "survival of the fittest," the evolutionary theory may one day act to determine the fit and unfit, the survivors and those who must offer their lives for the betterment of society.

Obviously no one knows if society will one day encourage the premature death of those perceived to be burdens. Yet one thing is very certain: the more we devalue life, the closer we get to such a reality.

Regardless of the direction man is heading, God is real. And in His eyes, the physically impaired are a unique, yet normal group of people. They are unique because, as magnificent men, they are distinct from animals. They are "normal" because like all other men, they are created in God's image. Thus, they and their lives are of great worth and worthy of true respect.

When you look in the mirror, what do you see? Do you see the remnants of a highly evolved ape or something much greater? I see a magnificent man created in the image of God. I see all men, impaired and unimpaired, maintaining great dignity and worth. What do you see? New reality or old, the choice is yours.

2 Who Sinned?

When considering the presence of the physically impaired, seldom do we give much thought to the origin or relevance of the impairment itself. This leaves us guessing as to the hows and whys of such things. Consequently, we are not positioned to fully appreciate the dynamics surrounding such things apart from working through these important details.

To many people, experiencing a physical affliction is a random event with no rhyme or reason. Biblically speaking, this is not the case. Some people are not simply born "lucky," while others are not. The Bible teaches there is a divine prescription and oversight here. The prescription is witnessed throughout Scripture and identifies such things as the inception and root cause of all impairments. It also helps us understand why some are impaired while others are left unhindered.

For those who are physically impaired or who minister to people who are, this is wonderful news, for with it comes hope. Hope in the knowledge of why people suffer. Hope because there is justifiable cause behind every affliction. Hope in the opportunity to resolve internal conflict resulting from physical impairments.

Hope because there is a glorious end to the physical and emotional strife that accompanies this cruel labor.

A glimpse of this hope is seen when Jesus and His disciples happened across a man who was born blind. The encounter led the disciples to ask Jesus, "Rabbi, who sinned, this man or his parents, that he was born blind?" Jesus answered, "Neither this man nor his parents sinned, but that the works of God should be revealed in him" (John 9:2-3).

It is evident from the disciples' question that they believed the blind man's impairment was the result of sin committed either in the womb or by his parents before he was born. This sort of thinking was common in that day. It was based on the presupposition that most, if not all, afflictions could be traced to some sort of personal sin.

While there is nothing to indicate that an unborn child is capable of sinning, there is biblical evidence to link physical impairment with sin. Scripture identifies at least five avenues in which sin may contribute to various impairments—three are witnessed in this passage.

The Person

The first avenue identified by the disciples was that of the person himself. The disciples asked Jesus, "Rabbi, who sinned, this man?" Jesus, knowing the heart of the blind man, dispelled the notion that the impairment was due to some sort of pre-birth sin.

In spite of Jesus' pronouncement, Scripture does acknowledge the presence of a sin nature within us prior to birth (Psalm 51:5; 58:3). This nature inclines man's heart toward sin. Therefore, even though Jesus discounted the occurrence of a pre-birth sin, Scripture as a whole supports the concept that a person's post-birth sin may contribute to a physical impairment.

The Bible presents two ways in which a person can obtain an impairment due to a personal sin. The first centers around the natural processes of life. Simply put, if someone commits a willful sin or partakes in questionable activities, such things may result in extreme illness, physical infirmities, or even death.

For example, those taking part in multi-partner sexual intercourse (Exodus 20:14; Leviticus 18:20-23; 20:10-16) are more likely to contract a sexually transmitted disease than people who practice abstinence or maintain a biblically based marriage. Those who regularly drive under the influence of mind-altering drugs or high levels of alcohol (Ephesians 5:18) have a higher probability of being seriously injured in an accident than those who do not.

One of the most well-known examples of this is seen in the life of baseball legend Mickey Mantle. He was a man who had it all, yet early in his career he became a heavy drinker. For roughly forty years he embraced this destructive lifestyle, and in June of 1995 his actions caught up with him—his liver was ruined by cancer. In an attempt to save his life, Mantle received a liver transplant. This proved futile, as the cancer had spread to other parts of his body. Months later Mickey died (Romans 6:21).

Another example is seen in the life of Samson. In word, mighty Samson was "a Nazirite to God from my mother's womb" (Judges 16:17), but in deed, he craved illicit relationships with godless women. One day Samson met a woman called Delilah, and he fell in love with her (Judges 16:4).

This was a fatal mistake because Delilah loved wealth more than she cared for Samson. Thus, she agreed to help the Philistines, one of his greatest enemies, capture him.

Delilah, cunning as a snake, coaxed Samson into revealing the source of his great strength. Once she determined his strength was linked to his hair, she babied him off to sleep and had a man "shave off the seven locks of his head" (Judges 16:19). Shortly after Samson awoke, he was seized by the Philistines and they mercilessly "put out his eyes" (Judges 16:21).

Samson, the strongest of men, was overpowered not by Delilah, nor by the Philistines, but by his own sinful desires. Time and time again, he chose to feed his sexual appetite rather than obey God's Word. As a result of his sinful behavior, Samson was left physically impaired.

Regardless of who we are, the principle remains the same. If we play with fire, we could get burned. If we flirt with certain types of sin, we may end up physically impaired. Why? Because some sins court tragic endings. God in His wisdom warns us of the dangers, but refuses to program our response. He created man in His image and grants us the ability to choose right from wrong. If we ignore God and His warnings, when tragedy befalls us we will have no one to blame but ourselves.

Thankfully, in most cases, God graciously shelters us from the full impact of honorless decisions. Nonetheless, at times He allows us to reap the full impact of what we have sown (Galatians 6:7).

The second way a person may obtain an impairment due to personal sin is by means of God's miraculous hand smiting the individual. It is important to note that this does not occur often. Given our propensity to commit acts of sin, if God impaired us every time we sinned, all of us would bear a multitude of physical scars denoting our foolishness. However, the Bible does contain many examples of sinful actions resulting in some sort of physical impairment.

We see a clear example of this when Moses' sister, Miriam, spoke against him. Apparently, she and her brother Aaron were bothered by Moses' decision to marry a Cushite woman. In their disgust they spoke against him. This was a terrible mistake, for their irreverence angered the Lord to the point of striking Miriam's body with leprosy. Once the leprosy was noticed, Aaron cried out to Moses, "Oh, my lord! Please do not lay this sin on us, in which we have done foolishly and in which we have sinned" (Numbers 12:11). The impairment caused both Aaron and Miriam to realize the gravity of their sin and turn from it.

In similar manner, God afflicted King Jeroboam with an impairment when he attempted to seize a prophet of God. He did so because he was angered by the prophet's prediction of future abominations King Josiah would commit roughly three hundred years later. Jeroboam's attempt to suppress the prophet resulted in God miraculously causing his hand to wither (1 Kings 13:4). This forced Jeroboam to humble himself and ask the prophet to pray (1 Kings 13:6) that God would restore his hand.

In both cases, we see the cause of God's miraculous affliction being the rebellious behavior of select individuals. When God afflicted these people He wasn't trying to be mean or oppressive, but was encouraging the offenders to recognize their sin and turn from it. God does not initiate such drastic measures without cause. Rather, He does so to encourage sinners to recognize their wrong and correct it immediately.

The Parents

The second avenue the disciples mentioned was that of the parents. They said to Jesus, "Rabbi, who sinned, this man or his parents?" (John 9:2). As in the case of the pre-birth sin, Jesus concluded the man's blindness was not a result of his parents' sin.

Here, the Lord's conclusion was not meant to be a blanket statement. Jesus knew full well a parent's sin may effect whether a child is born physically impaired or not.

Clearly, the Bible supports the idea that under certain circumstances the sin of a parent may result in a child being born physically impaired or sickly. As in the case of an individual's sin, if a parent commits a sin that is potentially hazardous to his or her health or body, such activity may ultimately harm the child.

For instance, if a child's mother is an excessive drinker or drug user, her habit may cause birth defects. (See Ephesians 5:18.) It is also possible that the child of an incestuous relationship may be born impaired. (See Leviticus 18:6.)

One of the most gruesome examples of a mother's sin resulting in her child being born impaired is seen in a pamphlet titled "The Questions Most People Ask About Abortion." It says:

> I'm a housewife and a registered nurse from Jacksonville. I worked the 11 p.m. to 7 a.m. shift, and when we weren't busy, I'd go out to help with the newborns. One night I saw a bassinet outside the nursery. There was a baby in this bassinet—a crying, perfectly formed baby—but there was a difference in this child. She had been scalded. She was the child of a saline abortion. This little girl looked as if she had been put in a pot of boiling water.[1]

In a saline abortion a strong salt solution is injected into the sac where the unborn child resides and develops during pregnancy. The solution blankets the child's body, burning the outer layer of skin and harming the baby when it ingests the poison solution.

---

1. Excerpt from "The Questions Most People Ask About Abortion" by Melody Green Copyright: 1989 Last Days Ministries, All Rights Reserved. Go to lastdaysministries.org for additional information.

Examples like this, shocking as they may be, force us to acknowledge the strong tie between the actions of a parent and the potential effect those actions may have on the unborn child.

When considering the far-reaching effects of a parent's sinful behavior, we see a graphic portrayal displayed in the life of King David. The Bible refers to him as a man after God's own heart (1 Samuel 13:14). David truly loved, followed and worshiped God with all his heart. Sadly he allowed lust for the wife of Uriah (a soldier in David's army) to tempt him into an adulterous relationship. The currents of his sin would ripple for generations. The impact of his sin was also felt immediately.

Like so many before and after him, David failed to confess his sin to God. Instead, he attempted to hide it. But the sin could not be suppressed because Bathsheba conceived a child (2 Samuel 11:5). Try as he may, David could not cover his sin. And as is so often the case, one sin led to another.

After a failed attempt to encourage Uriah to sleep with his wife, David made arrangements to have him killed in battle. Once that was accomplished, David believed the matter settled, but God would not have it. He sent the prophet Nathan to confront David with his sin. Once David realized he had been caught did he confess, saying, "I have sinned against the Lord" (2 Samuel 12:13).

Because David confessed his sin to God, he was forgiven, but forgiveness could not alter the consequences that had already been set in motion. David was informed by the prophet that "the child also who is born to you shall surely die" (2 Samuel 12:14).

Soon after, David began to labor in earnest. "David therefore pleaded with God for the child, and David fasted and went in and lay all night on the ground" (2 Samuel 12:16). David hoped in his heart God would somehow reverse the evil he had initiated. But it was not to be; the child became sick and eventually died.

Through David's sad tale, we learn that the sinful behavior of a parent may have far-reaching effects on the health and welfare of a child. Be it the result of natural processes, a dangerous or unhealthy lifestyle, or even God's judgment, children at times suffer at the hands of their parents' foolishness. Therefore, it is absolutely essential that parents carefully weigh their decisions before acting on them. Sin, in and of itself, is hideous enough without letting it seep into the lives of the helpless.

The Predecessor

When the disciples questioned Jesus about the origin of the blind man's disability, it appears they were expecting to hear only one of two responses. To their surprise, Jesus answered, "Neither this man nor his parents sinned, but that the works of God should be revealed in him" (John 9:3).

Jesus announced to those gathered that neither the blind man nor his parents were responsible for the impairment. What a great relief this must have been. Surely, the man and his parents must have grappled with the possibility that one of them may have been the cause of the blindness. But with one simple word, Jesus dispelled the notion.

In doing so, by default, the ultimate source of this impairment was directed toward the predecessor of all men. Who is the predecessor? His name is Adam. Adam is the father of all humanity. He introduced sin to humanity and, in turn, physical impairments.

In Genesis 3:17-19 we see God informing Adam of the results of his sin. He said:

> Cursed is the ground for your sake; In toil you shall eat of it all the days of your life. Both thorns and thistles it shall bring forth for you, and you shall eat the herb of the field. In the sweat of your face you shall eat bread till you return to the ground, for out of it you were taken; for dust you are, and to dust you shall return.

Some people choose to blame all their sorrows on God, but the Lord did not force Adam to sin. Adam chose to sin. God does not enjoy human suffering. Impairments are not the product of some form of warped entertainment created by God. Rather, the evils of this world were brought on by man and continue to be passed along by him.

If Adam had not sinned, his offspring would not bear the scars of the fall. The Bible says, "Therefore, just as through one man sin entered the world, and death through sin, and thus death spread to all men, because all sinned" (Romans 5:12).

Adam's sin is the root cause for all the woes of this world. Had he not sinned, the world would not be under a curse. If he had not sinned, his offspring would not maintain a sin nature that encourages us to sin. If man were not under the curse of sin, there would be no suffering, no death, no physical impairments.

Every physical impairment, whether the result of an individual, parent, or some other reason, may be linked to the person who brought the curse upon his people—Adam!

In the beginning, God created all things perfect. He provided man with everything he needed to make life pleasant. God refused to create a robot rather than a man. As a result, when God warned man not to sin and explained its consequences (Genesis 2:16-17), man had the ability to choose his course of action. Adam chose to sin.

Some might say, "Is it fair that we must suffer on account of our first father's actions?" The fact is, there is nothing fair about sin. Sin is man's enemy and it seeks to devour him. There is no goodness or fairness with sin. It is always tragic when innocent people suffer. Yet sin does not free, it oppresses. It does not heal, it harms. Sin cheats, steals, murders, lies, hurts, and leaves some people physically impaired. It is only by the grace of God that sin does not have greater sway upon humanity.

Those who struggle with physical impairments must not see God as a foe, but as their gracious and loving Friend. Adam is the root cause of the trials we now experience. Thus, when we encounter frustration, depression, hurt, and pain, let us remember it was Adam who brought this upon us, but it is the Lord who has worked to overcome it on our behalf.

The Patron

Another avenue we must consider is that of the patron. A patron is a follower or supporter of someone or something. In the case of the blind man, God elected him to be a patron on His behalf.

When the Lord announced to His disciples "that the works of God should be revealed in him," He was making it clear that some physical impairments are present for the purpose of demonstrating God's ministry to mankind.

God saw fit to use the man's blindness to illustrate His grace and matchless power. By healing him, Jesus nonverbally proclaimed that He truly desired to minister to the weak and needy, regardless of their plight. Unlike many others, He was capable of backing up His claim. As the Son of God, He could do what others could not—turn darkness into light.

We see a more powerful example of patronage in the life of Job. He was a man so completely in harmony with God and His Word that Satan yearned to devour him.

At the height of his battle with Job, Satan said to the Lord, "Skin for skin. . . . Yes, all that a man has he will give for his life. But stretch out Your hand now, and touch his bone and his flesh, and he will surely curse You to Your face!" (Job 2:4-5)

Satan hit the nail on the head! He realized the impact a severe impairment could have on men. He knew full well that when afflicted, most turn from God, blaming and cursing Him for it.

Satan longed to hear Job cry out curses upon God. He hungered for the moment when Job would turn from the Lord and deny Him the glory He deserved. He felt that if he could push Job just a little further, Job would self-destruct and give in. Satan wrongly believed that it was impossible for a mere human to overcome such an obstacle.

Sadly, there are many who fit Satan's understanding of humanity. They treat God as if He is the cause of all their problems. When something goes wrong, they are quick to curse and deny Him. Perhaps they do so because they believe this is just treatment for an unjust God. But the man who responds in this manner has allowed himself to be deceived, for God is not the root cause of man's problems. Adam's sin infected humanity with the curse, not God. And it is Satan who roams the earth looking for those he may ensnare, not the Lord.

Unlike the vast majority of people, when Satan's darts came hurling toward him, Job refused to cower. The Bible says, "So Satan went out from the presence of the Lord, and struck Job with painful boils from the sole of his foot to the crown of his head" (Job 2:7). Job was in great agony, impaired from head to toe. In his commentary on the book of Job, Matthew Henry said:

> One boil, when it is gathering, is torment enough, and gives a man abundance of pain and uneasiness. What a condition was Job then in, that had boils all over him, and no part free, and those of as raging a heat as the devil could make them, and, as it were, set on fire of hell![2]

Surely this dear patron suffered mightily at the hands of the aggressor. But regardless of the affliction, as true as gold, Job continued to honor God.

Unfortunately, the more he persevered, the more Satan sought to trip him up. Job, a man who had already suffered immeasurable loss, found himself assailed by "painful boils" from head to toe—reaping the scathing wrath of the devil's hatred.

As the patron quietly rested in the ashes, scraping himself with a piece of broken pottery, his wife came to him, crying out, "Do you still hold fast to your integrity? Curse God and die!" (Job 2:9). As difficult as it must have been, Job once more fought off temptation and replied, "You speak as one of the foolish women speaks. Shall we indeed accept good from God, and shall we not accept adversity?" (Job 2:10). "Of course not" begs to be heard, but silence was her only response.

Try as he might, Satan could not bait Job into denouncing God. Without realizing it, Job single-handedly overcame the serpent of old. As the truest of patrons, this mighty saint offered up one of the most glorious gifts a person can give their Lord—victory over His ancient foe.

Of all the great men of God, Job may be the most splendid patron! Many have suffered at the hands of Satan, and many have overcome, but few have been pushed as far as Job was. Clearly he was pushed for one reason: to bear out the Lord's presence and ministry in his life by glorifying Him through his suffering. And that is exactly what he did. Job is a model for all those called to stand as patrons on God's behalf.

The Populace

The question of why some people are born physically impaired and others are afflicted later in life is a very important one. Indeed, many in this world suffer from one impairment or another.

As we have seen, sometimes afflictions are brought on as a result of a person or their parents' sin. At times, it's Satan knock-

---

2. Matthew Henry, *Matthew Henry's Commentary*, Volume III, p. 14.

ing at our door. Likewise, there are times when afflictions can only be viewed as an outgrowth of Adam's sin. Regardless of the source, the potential variables one must consider when contemplating the presence of impairments or afflictions are numerous to say the least.

For the sake of providing balance, the Bible offers an additional explanation. It appears when Jesus was entertaining questions from a crowd of people. Some of those present "told Him about the Galileans whose blood Pilate had mingled with their sacrifices" (Luke 13:1). Jesus took that opportunity to further the group's understanding of human tragedy, saying:

> Do you suppose that these Galileans were worse sinners than all other Galileans, because they suffered such things? I tell you, no . . . Or those eighteen on whom the tower in Siloam fell and killed them, do you think that they were worse sinners than all other men who dwelt in Jerusalem? I tell you, no (Luke 13:2-5).

Here the Lord helps us understand that not all suffering, pain, torment, and death are the result of immediate sin. At times, for unknown reasons, the general populace is hurt, impaired, or even killed. The cause is not some sort of personal sin they or their parents have committed, nor because Satan is "after them." Rather, it is simply an indication that we are living in a world that is passing away. Cars crash, towers decay and fall to the ground, injustices occur, and at times we find ourselves in the wrong place at the wrong time.

When Jesus spoke of the Galileans and the "eighteen on whom the tower in Siloam fell," His observation applied to all people, both believers and nonbelievers alike. Essentially, Jesus was letting us know that bad things can happen to good people.

Clearly, the only good that comes from such things is that they continually remind us that this world is not our home. Just as the tower in Siloam fell, this world is falling apart. For that reason, each of us must make a choice. We may embrace a lost and dying world in the midst of decay, or opt for a heavenly home impervious to such things. We can fix our hope on the steadiness of the "tower in Siloam," or we may set our frail frames upon the solid rock of Christ. Where is your hope fixed? On the "tower" or on the rock?

> My hope is built on nothing less, then Jesus' blood and righteousness; I dare not trust the sweetest frame, But wholly lean on Jesus' name. On Christ, the solid Rock, I stand; All other ground is sinking sand, All other ground is sinking sand.[3]

Everyone is susceptible to having their blood "mingled with their sacrifices" (Luke 13:1). No one, no matter how good or bad, is exempt from the "tower in Siloam" potentially falling on him. Each of us needs life insurance—eternal life insurance. That is the only thing we can count on. Whether your physical impairment is self-inflicted, brought on by parents, or from some other avenue, there is no guarantee against suffering. Nevertheless, Christ died to guarantee eternal life for all those who embrace it.

Reality Balanced

There are many reasons why people experience physical impairments. At times God uses such things to punish us or to get our attention, but as we have seen, this is rare. More often than not impairments are simply a by-product of sin's effect upon this world.

The Lord also uses physical impairments as an instrument of teaching. He teaches us many things through them. We learn of His sovereignty, graciousness, loving kindness, and mercy. Through impairments He teaches us about the effects of sin upon mankind, accountability, holiness, and judgment. We are taught of the fierceness of spiritual warfare and how Satan uses impairments as a mighty weapon against the inhabitants of this world. Most important the Lord teaches us that we can use physical impairments to honor and glorify Him through our personal examples.

As heartbreaking as an impairment may be, we are called to view such reality through God's Word. Therefore, we must strive

---

3. Edward Mote, The Solid Rock, *Great Hymns of The Faith*, p. 272.

to see impairments as God sees them. We must recognize that with these tragedies comes some good. Likewise, when faced with the trials impairments bring, rather than focusing on the momentary picture, we must strive to view reality from an eternal perspective. The Bible says we are to "walk by faith, not by sight" (2 Corinthians 5:7). Consequently, through a balanced understanding of reality, we are to view impairments not through the frail framework of man, but through God's eternal vantage point.

3 The Thorn

In God's hands, physical impairments and afflictions are much like the thorns gathered around the stem of a beautiful rose. Although they may be sharp and painful to the touch, the Lord can use them to bring about some important results in our lives. Let's take a brief look at five ways in which the Lord can use impairments or afflictions to further us spiritually.

Enforcement

At times in Scripture, God uses various impairments or afflictions to enforce His commandments. Paul established this concept while warning the Corinthians not to wrongly partake in the Lord's Supper. He said:

> Therefore whoever eats this bread or drinks this cup of the Lord in an unworthy manner will be guilty of the body and blood of the Lord. But let a man examine himself, and so let him eat of the bread and drink of the cup. For he who eats and drinks in an unworthy manner eats and drinks judgment to himself, not discerning the Lord's body. For this reason many

are weak and sick among you, and many sleep. For if we would judge ourselves, we would not be judged. But when we are judged, we are chastened by the Lord, that we may not be condemned with the world. (1 Corinthians 11:27-32)

Apparently some of the Corinthians were partaking of the Lord's Supper in an "unworthy manner." In God's eyes this constituted sinful behavior, for they acted disrespectfully toward the commemoration of Christ's death. Rather than allowing the people to do as they pleased, God called them to account for their actions.

The Lord exacted judgment on the people by causing "many" to become "weak and sick" and even to "sleep" (die). The exact cause of the weakness, sickness, and death is unknown, but God did not hesitate to use these tools to reprove the wayward.

The Lord exhibited this high level of discipline as a means of nonverbally warning the people. It was His way of telling them they had committed a serious sin.

Stop and Take Notice

This leads us to ask why God uses such things to enforce His commands? There are many reasons, but one of the most practical is to help us stop and take notice.

When our youngest child, Joy, was one year old, my wife decided to teach her not to disassemble our plants. Initially my wife lightly slapped her on the hand. But Joy refused to heed the gentle reminders; therefore, my wife slapped her hand a little harder. Yet she paid little attention until the slaps became painful. Whether young or old, the outcome is often the same. Words are meaningless if no one is listening.

The church of Corinth knew better than to act disrespectfully. Yet due to spiritual immaturity they approached the Lord's Supper irreverently. As a result, some became "weak"—a gentle slap on the church's "hand." Others became "sick"—a firmer slap. Finally a number fell asleep (died)—a very painful slap on the church's hand. In essence, God was saying, "If you are going to act like children, I am going to treat you like children."

Why would God do this? Initially, to help the church stop and take notice, but ultimately He sought to move the congregation from a negative circumstance to a more positive one.

As with the Corinthians, the Lord does not reprove us because He is mean and nasty, but rather to encourage us to maintain obedience to His Word. As our Creator and eternal Father, He knows what is best for us, and He has gone to great lengths to make such things evident. The Bible says, "To obey is better than sacrifice" (1 Samuel 15:22). In other words, we may choose to offer everything we possess to the Lord, yet if we lack obedience, our gifts are meaningless. Jesus said, "If you love Me, keep My commandments" (John 14:15). Obedience, not giving, is the greatest act of love one can display toward God, for true giving is an outgrowth of obedience.

The Lord's reproof is also a means of encouraging us to live a life of purity. The remedy Paul offered the Corinthians is self-examination. He said, "Let a man examine himself, and so let him eat of the bread and drink of the cup" (1 Corinthians 11:28). What is the goal of self-examination? Purity. If the apostle's words are heeded, a sense of self-accountability will exist in the lives of believers. Ultimately, this should lead to the recognition of personal sin, followed by repentance (turning from the sin) and restoration.

Why is this important? Because as 1 John 3:3 notes, "Everyone who has this hope in Him purifies himself, just as He is pure." When impurity reigns in our hearts, we are incapable of pleasing God (Proverbs 28:9).

The end product of God's encouragement culminates in respect for Him. If the Corinthians maintained godly obedience and a sense of Christlike purity, respect for Him would be present.

Perhaps the greatest reason the Corinthians were plagued by afflictions was due to their disrespect. One would think all believers would come to the Lord's Table reverently, but that simply is not so. Therefore, in the case of the Corinthians, God sought to encourage them to obedience, purity, and respectfulness through weakness, sickness, and even death.

Love

The second reason the Lord uses impairments to enforce His commands is that He loves us. This may sound strange to some, but Scripture says, "My son, do not despise the chastening of the

Lord, nor detest His correction; for whom the Lord loves He corrects" (Proverbs 3:11-12). At times, the Lord uses impairments or afflictions as a means of discipline. We have already seen examples of this in the lives of people like David, Miriam, and Jeroboam.

How can the Bible equate "chastening" with "love"? Scripture recognizes that true discipline seeks the restoration of the wayward—when discipline is heeded, one is able to avoid the many pitfalls brought on by waywardness. Causing someone to confront and thereby avoid destructive behavior is an act of love.

During the 1994 Winter Olympics, CBS television featured a downhill skier named Tommy Moe. As a teenager, Tommy was a terrific skier, but he was very rebellious and undisciplined. His problem was so enormous he was eventually expelled from the ski team.

When Tommy arrived home, his father realized he had a major problem on his hands. He knew if he did not correct the problem soon, his son would ruin his life. As owner of a construction company, Tommy's dad was able to put him to work immediately. Tommy was made to work from early morning to late evening, six days a week.

After two months of hard labor, his dad asked him if he wanted to continue as is or go back to skiing. Eagerly he went back to skiing. Years later, after winning the Olympic gold medal, Tommy said he would never have won apart from his father's loving act of discipline.

Love and discipline are compatible. The Lord chastens those He loves. Scripture says, "Now no chastening seems to be joyful for the present, but painful; nevertheless, afterward it yields the peaceable fruit of righteousness to those who have been trained by it" (Hebrews 12:11).

From a human perspective, discipline is painful. Initially, it is not welcomed. But as time passes, for those who humble themselves before the Lord, "it yields the peaceable fruit of righteousness." This harvest helps us become more like God—reaping a harvest that helps us find peace amid the trials of life, and through it comes hope and a measure of precious revival to our souls.

When confronted by God's hand of discipline it is essential to remember that "God is love" (1 John 4:8).

Entanglement

When men sin, they often attempt to conceal it. Most of us would rather sweep our sin under a rug than face up to it. This is a result of pride and displays our distaste for recognizing and confessing the wrongs we have committed.

Because of our pride, God sometimes uses impairments and afflictions to entangle us with our wrongdoings. This is a result of a system of checks and balances God has established. The apostle Paul brought this to light when he said:

> Do not be deceived, God is not mocked; for whatever a man sows, that he will also reap. For he who sows to his flesh will of the flesh reap corruption, but he who sows to the Spirit will of the Spirit reap everlasting life. (Galatians 6:7-8)

The principle of moral sowing and reaping, as seen in Galatians, acts as an indicator of our eternal standing before the Lord. Specifically, the concept of sowing and reaping reminds us that we are accountable to God for our actions. If we disobey Him, He has every right to demand us to endure the consequences of our actions.

The Lord's primary objective is to encourage us to carefully weigh our decisions prior to acting on them, and thereby align our responses with the clear teaching of Scripture. Through obedience to God's Word, we affirm our relationship with Him. Failure, on the other hand, creates the potential for all sorts of havoc.

We see an example of this in the life of Herod Agrippa I. While in Caesarea, the people of Tyre and Sidon met with him. Apparently there had been some strife between Herod and the two cities—nonetheless, the people now sought peace.

During the course of their meeting, in an effort to win Herod's favor, the people shouted, "The voice of a god and not of a man!" (Acts 12:22) Herod, being very prideful, accepted the praise and status reserved exclusively for God.

The historian Josephus says, upon accepting the praise, Herod "felt a stab of pain in his heart. He was also gripped in his stomach by an ache that he felt everywhere at once." Herod attributed his impairment to God, saying, "I, who was called immortal by you, am now under the sentence of death. But I must accept my lot as God will it."[1] And indeed he did—Herod suffered for five days, and then died.

Herod's dramatic affliction was exceptional, yet necessary to prove God's willingness to allow man to become entangled with the consequences of his sin. Why does the Lord allow such things to happen? Because they affirm the seriousness of wrongful behavior. For some, affliction acts as a reminder of why godliness is essential. For others, it scares them into correct behavior. For many, it acts as an indicator of their eternal fate. In any case, entanglement in such things broadcasts the sobering message that God is alive and very concerned with our actions and attitudes. This God, like it or not, holds us accountable for all we say and do.

Equality

A third purpose physical impairment serves is to bear witness to the equality of God. When things go wrong, people are quick to blame God and question His fairness. But above all else, God is equitable.

The Bible bears this out when it says, "He makes His sun rise on the evil and on the good, and sends rain on the just and on the unjust" (Matthew 5:45).

Unlike man, God is impartial. At birth, the children of both friend and foe are born impaired and unimpaired. During the course of life, both the just and unjust take on physical impairments and afflictions. Such things are glaring examples of the extent God will go to maintain equity.

The Lord does not hypocritically command us to "love your enemies" (Matthew 5:44) while ignoring that command Himself. Rather, on a daily basis, billions of expressions of love are directed toward those who hate and ignore Him.

Yes, God allows afflictions to come upon His enemies, but He allows the same impairments to come upon His friends. Who else in the annals of time has been more equitable than God? His fairness cannot be challenged. For centuries, He has allowed His ene-

---

1. Paul L. Maier (ed.), *Josephus - The Essential Writings*, p. 272.

mies to spit upon His name, while providing them with the saliva to do so!

The Lord could very well put a hedge around His saints, allowing the curse of Adam's sin to plague only His enemies. But the God of fairness and equity "makes His sun rise on the evil and on the good," and physical impairments and afflictions on the just and unjust.

Edification

Seldom do we consider physical impairments and afflictions as serving a positive purpose. But in a very real way, the presence of an impairment can assist in the edification of a believer. Charles Hodge, a prominent theologian from the nineteenth century, said, "The experience of God's people shows that bodily pain has a special office to perform in the work of sanctification."[2]

Dr. Hodge was correct in his assertion. In the life of the apostle Paul, God used this vehicle to minister to him. Paul established this when he said:

> And lest I should be exalted above measure by the abundance of the revelations, a thorn in the flesh was given to me, a messenger of Satan to buffet me, lest I be exalted above measure. Concerning this thing I pleaded with the Lord three times that it might depart from me. And He said to me, "My grace is sufficient for you, for My strength is made perfect in weakness." Therefore most gladly I will rather boast in my infirmities, that the power of Christ may rest upon me. Therefore I take pleasure in infirmities, in reproaches, in needs, in persecutions, in distresses, for Christ's sake. For when I am weak, then I am strong. (2 Corinthians 12:7-10)

The "edification" of a saint denotes the building up or strengthening of the person spiritually. Specifically, the term centers around the building up of a believer in the knowledge and understanding of God's Word. But in a more general sense, it includes all aspects of the Christian walk.

---

2. Charles Hodge, *The Geneva Series of Commentaries I & II Corinthians*, p. 662.

A concrete example of this is seen in the "thorn" Paul spoke of. Over the centuries, there has been much debate as to its identity. For sake of argument, we will assume it to be some sort of physical impairment or affliction.

When such things enter the life of a believer, they are sometimes present to serve a special purpose, as in Paul's case. Often they serve as a means of strengthening and building up a believer. When this is the case, what are some of the potential benefits one may derive?

Focus

When an impairment enters the life of a committed believer, it encourages him or her to focus on the Lord. Upon recognition of his problem, how did Paul respond? He turned to the Lord for help. Paul said, "I pleaded with the Lord three times that it might depart from me" (2 Corinthians 12:8).

By going to the Lord three times, Paul expressed the seriousness of the problem. This was obviously no small matter to him. Initially, Paul appeared to be shaken by the occurrence, as he pleaded for its removal.

Undoubtedly, the impairment acted as a magnet, drawing and focusing Paul's attention on God. More than anything else, during times of stress and difficulty the Lord wants us to focus on Him through prayer.

By going to Him, we establish the depth of our faith in Him. During times like these, some people tend to avoid God. Others, like a soldier under fire, may seek His deliverance; yet when the threat passes so does their commitment. Regardless of one's choice, during times of trouble, there is only One we can or should set our sights on: the Lord Jesus.

Perspective

A second thing an impairment reinforces is a proper perspective. When faced with the enormity of an impairment, a reality check may accompany it. Times like these may reveal the true disposition of our view of reality and in turn uncover the source of our personal motivation.

If we view reality only through man's limited perspective, we are setting ourselves up for a fall. Man's perspective is always limited to the small and momentary picture. Man has a bad case of tunnel vision. When trials come our way, we often see only what we choose to see, while ignoring all else.

The apostle was greatly concerned with his impairment, but he realized his perspective was limited. As a result, he went to God in prayer. Indeed, Paul desired the removal of the "thorn," but sought its removal with a balanced perspective. He not only petitioned God, but listened for His response as well. And how did God respond? "My grace is sufficient for you, for My strength is made perfect in weakness" (2 Corinthians 12:9).

Impairments and afflictions cause us to realize our perspective is lacking, while God's is complete. As humans, we are only able to comprehend the few grains of sand that personally influence us. God not only grasps every granule, but the entire beach as well. Thus, the wisest thing we can do is follow Paul's example. Like the apostle, we must take our concerns to the Lord and then be prepared to yield to His response.

Reliance

The natural response of those who maintain a proper focus and godly perspective is a balanced reliance on the Lord. It is natural because they have grasped the reality of God's superiority through personal interaction with Him. As a result, confidence and trust in Him is built and extended.

Those maintaining a degree of biblical wisdom are pressed in this direction, for they have come to realize the obvious—God is in control and all things under heaven are reliant on Him.

Even though Paul longed to have the "thorn" removed, he recognized his reliance on the Lord. Thus, rather than opposing God, he proclaimed, "Therefore most gladly I will rather boast in my infirmities, that the power of Christ may rest upon me" (2 Corinthians 12:9). The apostle acknowledged God's sovereignty over his impairment and accordingly entrusted it into His care.

We also see that Paul recognized the source of his strength and empowerment: the Lord. In his wisdom he realized that to resist the Lord would adversely influence other areas of his life—

whereas wholehearted submission and dependence would solidify Christ's strength upon him. Thus, Paul responded with heartfelt approval.

Yes, it is true we have the freedom to scoff at God and attempt to go it alone, but this is the way of the fool. Scripture says, "The fool has said in his heart, 'There is no God'" (Psalm 14:1). The fool, in his antlike world, deludes himself into believing there is no God. By doing so, the fool hopes to circumvent accountability and dependence on God. The problem is, a billion fools believing with all their hearts that God does not exist or is not sovereign over them does not alter the truth. The only thing denial or rejection accomplishes is postponing the inevitable.

> For we shall all stand before the judgment seat of Christ. For it is written: "As I live, says the Lord, Every knee shall bow to Me, and every tongue shall confess to God." (Romans 14:10-11)

Secular newspapers may proclaim "God is dead," but one day those proclaiming such things will weep bitterly over their words. But those who find their sustenance and reliance in God will joyously proclaim forever "He is alive!"

Joyfulness

True reliance on the Lord encourages the impaired to enter a state of joyfulness. Like most people, Paul chose to pray and plead for the removal of the "thorn." When the Lord responded in a contrary manner, Paul could have sulked, gotten angry, or even turned on God. But instead, the fruit of joyfulness was produced in Paul's heart. He said, "I take pleasure" (2 Corinthians 12:10).

How is it possible to be joyful when afflicted with a life-changing impairment? Do as Paul did! Focus on the Lord. View reality from God's perspective. Rely on Him, for He is in control. Apart from this, Paul would have responded the same as anyone else. He would have been a pitiful mess.

This is not to say that the faithful never struggle. Initially, Paul struggled with the impairment. He pleaded for it to be removed. Yet the important thing to keep in mind is not the initial struggle, but the ultimate victory and joy that followed.

Maturity

A vital result of those who triumph over trials created by physical impairment is spiritual maturity. Paul displayed this when he said, "Therefore I take pleasure in infirmities, in reproaches, in needs, in persecutions, in distresses, for Christ's sake" (2 Corinthians 12:10).

We see a similar response from young David Brainerd, a missionary to the New England Indians in the eighteenth century.

> Oh, that I might always be perfectly quiet in seasons of greatest weakness, although nature should sink and fail! Oh, that I may always be able with utmost sincerity to say, "Lord, not my will, but thine be done!" This, through grace, I can say at present with regard to life or death, "The Lord do with me as seems good in his sight"; that whether I live or die, I may glorify Him, who is "worthy to receive blessing, and honor, and dominion forever. Amen."[3]

During Brainerd's years of ministry, his life was constantly threatened by hostile Indians and severe illness. Thus, when he speaks of "seasons of greatest weakness" he is not simply mouthing empty words. When echoing the sentiments "The Lord do with me as seems good in his sight; that whether I live or die," he meant every word of it.

After many years of torturous winters and great hardships, his body could no longer go on. Young David died October 10, 1747, at the tender age of thirty-two.

David Brainerd, like the great apostle, matured as a result of the challenges impairments and afflictions brought. As Christians, did they struggle? Of course! But more importantly they overcame!

These men clearly exhibited the badge of spiritual maturity. Both lived and died seeking to glorify God—and oh, how they did so!

There is nothing wonderful about carrying the burden of a physical impairment, but as we have seen, wonderful things can

---

3. Jonathan Edwards, (ed.) *The Life and Diary of David Brainerd*, p. 333.

result from their presence in our lives. As we face the trials of physical impairment, or seek to minister to those who are impaired, let us remember the Pauls and Davids who have gone before us. Like them, we may struggle and plead with God, but I pray that like them, we may also mature and be built up in the faith.

Exaltation

In a day when personal pleasure stands high on the totem pole of life, few see any benefit in humbly weathering the afflictions. Regardless of such an outlook, there remains one additional benefit gained through physical impairment: exaltation.

The Believer in Christ

John Bunyan, seventeenth-century author of *Pilgrim's Progress*, was a man familiar with the trials of human suffering. Bunyan spent twelve years in prison because of his preaching. He once said:

> I have often thought that the best of Christians are found in the worst times: and I have thought again, that one reason why we are not better is, because God purges us no more. Noah and Lot, who so holy as they in the time of their afflictions! and yet, who so idle as they in the time of their prosperity?[4]

Bunyan realized something few today dare consider: that spiritual prosperity and personal exaltation may be gained via personal affliction. In a very real sense, his observation was repeatedly played out throughout Scripture.

Suffering and exaltation can work together in the life of a believer. The Bible speaks of the faithful saints of the Old Testament who chose to undergo terrible suffering on behalf of their faith.

> Still others had trial of mockings and scourgings, yes, and of chains and imprisonment. They were stoned, they were sawn

---

4. John Bunyan, *The Riches of John Bunyan*, p. 273.

in two, were tempted, were slain with the sword. They wandered about in sheepskins and goatskins, being destitute, afflicted, tormented—of whom the world was not worthy. They wandered in deserts and mountains, in dens and caves of the earth. (Hebrews 11:36-38)

Why would anyone in his right mind allow himself to undergo such trials? Scripture says, "that they might obtain a better resurrection" (Hebrews 11:35). These faithful saints endured hardships not to receive honor from man, but to be exalted by God.

They longed to be exalted come eternity. They longed to hear the words, "Well done, good and faithful servant. . . . Enter into the joy of your lord" (Matthew 25:21). What they did, they did to please and honor their Master.

Today, we may not grasp the magnitude of such things, but like the saints of old, afflictions and suffering will pale in comparison to the exaltation we will experience. From an eternal perspective, trials, physical impairments, and personal suffering are little compared to the glory the faithful will one day experience.

Paul said, "Even though our outward man is perishing, yet the inward man is being renewed day by day. For our light affliction, which is but for a moment, is working for us a far more exceeding and eternal weight of glory" (2 Corinthians 4:16-17). Is there hope in these words? Is there exaltation? There is enough to strengthen the weariest of souls.

How is this possible? Because for those truly grounded in the faith, battles such as these take on new significance. Paul made this clear when he said, "Therefore I take pleasure in infirmities, in reproaches, in needs, in persecutions, in distresses, for Christ's sake. For when I am weak, then I am strong" (2 Corinthians 12:10).

There is strength in weakness if our source is the "power of Christ" (2 Corinthians 12:9)—for through Christ we turn from self-reliance to reliance in God.

To the faithful saint, afflictions and personal suffering are as hot coals. These coals are stoked through the power of Christ. The combination acts as a mighty fuel that creates an inner fire of personal commitment. This works to raise up eternal flames of glory and godly success.

The strength Paul speaks of is available to all. But in order to gain it, we must allow ourselves to be fueled by Christ's power, not our own. We must see trials, impairments, and suffering as opportunities to rest in the grace that was sufficient for Paul and continues to be sufficient for us as well.

The Lord

The ultimate form of exaltation we may partake in is that of glorifying the Lord. We may glorify Him in many ways. Most commonly He is exalted through words of praise, prayer, and song, but He is likewise exalted through our lives.

Glorifying God through our lives finds its roots in a living and active commitment to Him. True commitment commences within the heart and graduates into every aspect of our being. As a result, the Lord is exalted inwardly by our thoughts, desires, emotions, and outwardly though our words, expressions, and actions.

Those who are physically impaired have a unique opportunity to exalt God through their lives, because they are pitied by people. Some people expect bitterness, resentment, anxiety, and depression from them because they have been "deprived" of things others take for granted. Therefore, many believe they have every reason to be dissatisfied with life.

Hardships provide an opportunity for the impaired to glorify God through their example. When the physically impaired offer up heartfelt praise, prayer, and song, the unimpaired have reason to listen. Why? Because if those who have experienced some of life's most difficult trials can exalt God, others who have not are without excuse. If the quadriplegic, the blind, and the lame can rejoice and show appreciation to God, there is little room for others to respond to the contrary.

Who can say to the physically impaired, "You glorify God only because your life is easy." No one, of course. Why? Because their lives are difficult and full of various trials and degrees of suffering. If they understand life's trials better than most, and yet glorify God, shouldn't we maintain a degree of appreciation for their selfless example?

The physically impaired, through lives of true commitment to God, have a wonderful opportunity to multiply all they do to His glory. The essence of their relationship with God and their absolute commitment to Him can speak volumes to those around them. Their lives can translate glory to God, while simultaneously posing a challenge for others to follow.

4 The Burdens

The presence of the physically impaired within the framework of the Bible adds color, dimension, and a sense of reality to God's Word. The impaired are not simply viewed as a passing thought; rather, they are an integral part of the Bible's makeup.

As we contemplate the presence of the physically impaired, we notice many examples of those burdened with some sort of impairment. Likewise, throughout Scripture we see a wide variety of impairments and afflictions.

Some of the impairments found in the Bible are not typically thought of as physical impairments. Yet for the sake of thoroughness, we will consider them under this heading.

Types of Physical Impairments

Generally speaking, the impairments mentioned in the Bible fall into three basic categories: Bodily Deficiencies, Irregularities, and Ailments.

These categories may be broken down into two subcategories. The first contains impairments that are natural or non-induced.

Their presence is an outgrowth of the common genetic or biological functions that regularly occur within humanity as a whole.

The second subcategory includes physical impairments that were acquired in a supernatural or induced manner. They originate from God, agents of God, demonics (demon possession or oppression), and the like.

Within these subcategories, Scripture speaks of impairments in both literal and figurative terms. When referring to impairments literally, the Bible often does so to help identify an actual physical condition maintained by a person. At times the Bible also mentions specific impairments for the purpose of instructing us how we should relate to them.

When referring to an impairment figuratively, the Bible often looks to expose a spiritual, theological, intellectual, or emotional problem a person or group of people exhibits. Its purpose is to present a vivid word picture establishing the essence of the problem. Thus, the imagery of the impairment acts to symbolize some type of literal flaw in the life of a person or group of people.

Bodily Deficiencies

The first category mentioned in the Bible is generally viewed as the most severe of those presented. It encompasses a wide range of impairments that tend to completely rob an individual of a body function or part.

Blindness

One of the most common impairments cited in the Bible is blindness. The condition is mentioned at least fifty-four times. It is used literally and figuratively. Literally, it denotes those who have partially or completely lost their eyesight. Figuratively, it depicts those who are spiritually or ethically lacking in their ability to comprehend something (See Deuteronomy 16:19; Matthew 15:14; 23:16; Romans 11:25; 2 Corinthians 3:14; 2 Peter 1:9.)

Blindness Brought on Naturally

The Bible presents many examples of natural blindness. In the Old Testament we see blindness due to old age in the lives of Eli

(1 Samuel 3:2) and Ahijah (1 Kings 14:4). Perhaps the most familiar example is Isaac's loss of vision due to old age. Scripture says, "Isaac was old and his eyes were so dim that he could not see" (Genesis 27:1). Sadly, Isaac's vision was so poor his son Jacob was able to fool him into believing he was his older brother, Esau. Jacob's deception allowed him to wrongly obtain a special blessing reserved for Esau.

In the New Testament we see Christ healing the blind (John 9:1-12). One case was a blind beggar called Bartimaeus (Mark 10:46). While sitting near the road begging, Bartimaeus heard Jesus passing by and began shouting to Him. When Jesus stopped to talk to him, He asked Bartimaeus what he wanted. Bartimaeus said, "Rabboni, that I may receive my sight." Jesus responded, "Go your way; your faith has made you well." The passage says, "Immediately he received his sight" (Mark 10:51-52). As in the case of Bartimaeus, on many occasions, Jesus proved He was Lord over the visual impairments of men.

Blindness Brought on Supernaturally

Scripture also provides several examples of blindness brought about supernaturally. One instance took place when the men of Sodom attempted to seize two angels residing with Lot (Abraham's nephew). The Bible says, the angels "struck the men who were at the doorway of the house with blindness" (Genesis 19:11). This encounter resulted in a temporary loss of sight, thus keeping the Sodomites from fulfilling their evil quest.

In another example God elected to blind men on behalf of a prophet. This occurred when Elisha asked God to blind the Arameans in order to prevent them from taking him captive (2 Kings 6:18). His plea resulted in the Arameans losing their sight and spared him from capture.

One of the most graphic pictures of induced blindness is Paul's loss of sight. There the risen Christ questioned Paul concerning his fierce persecution of the church. Once the Lord finished His examination, Paul was told to head to the city. Scripture says, "Saul arose from the ground, and when his eyes were opened he saw no one. But they led him by the hand and brought him into Damascus. And he was three days without sight" (Acts 9:8-9).

Without a doubt, Paul's loss of vision was directly caused by Christ. The significance of his blindness is unknown. Yet it appears it was God's way of getting Paul's complete attention. The point of such an attention-getter was to encourage a sense of spiritual sobriety. In light of this, after Paul's vision was restored, it's no surprise, "he arose and was baptized" (Acts 9:18). Clearly, when God wants to get someone's attention, He will use any means, including blindness, to do so.

God's Provision for the Blind

Even though blindness disallowed a man from the priesthood of Israel, this is not an indication of God's general disfavor. To illustrate, we need only consider God's special provision on behalf of the blind. Prior to crossing into the Promised Land, Moses instructed the people, saying, "Cursed is the one who makes the blind to wander off the road" (Deuteronomy 27:18). God was informing Israel to treat the blind courteously and with fairness. Those who failed to do so were "cursed" of God.

God's protective care of the blind bears witness to the importance such people hold in His eyes. By example, God encourages all men to treat the blind with fairness and respect.

Deafness and Dumbness

Two physical impairments that tend to be closely linked are deafness and dumbness (mutes). When the Bible speaks literally of deafness, it indicates someone with complete or near-complete loss of hearing. Dumbness refers to someone who is unable to speak or someone whose speech cannot be understood.

Typically, when the Bible uses the term figuratively, deafness denotes a person who is unwilling or unable to hear a message from God, His Word, or one of His spokesmen (Psalm 38:13; 58:4; Isaiah 42:19). Their lack is not physical, but spiritual.

When referring to dumbness figuratively, the Bible uses the word rather broadly. It is generally associated with some form of speechlessness (Psalm 39:1-2; Daniel 10:15 KJV). The impairment tends to be limited to a person's inability to verbally respond or defend himself, as opposed to lacking the ability to actually speak. In the case of idols (false gods created by man), it signifies a complete inability to communicate with man (Habakkuk 2:19; 1 Corinthians 12:2; Psalm 38:13-14; Isaiah 53:7; Acts 8:32 KJV).

Deafness and Dumbness Brought on Naturally

In the Bible we see no clear examples of non-induced deafness and dumbness. We can only presume the deaf and speech-impaired man in Mark 7:31-37 was born with these impairments, as their origin is not shared. We are also left to presume that some of the "deaf" spoken of in Luke 7:22 were born that way or developed the impairment over time.

Deafness and Dumbness Brought on Supernaturally

In the New Testament many examples of deafness and dumbness were attributed to demonics. At times we see Jesus directly confronting the demonic world seeking to cast out controlling spirits. In one case the Lord is seen casting out an evil spirit that had possessed a young man (Mark 9:14-28).

Within this account, we see a precise example of induced deafness and dumbness resulting from demon possession. We know this to be the case because the father of the boy said, "Teacher, I brought You my son, who has a mute [dumbness, unable to speak] spirit" (Mark 9:17). Through this statement we see the boy was not always speechless, but at some point he lost the ability.

Jesus affirmed the father's testimony by acknowledging the presence of the evil spirit, saying, "Deaf and dumb spirit, I command you, come out of him and enter him no more" (Mark 9:25). Scripture says, "Then the spirit cried out, convulsed him greatly, and came out of him" (Mark 9:26). As a direct result of Jesus' command, the evil spirit immediately left the boy.

Beyond demon possession, the Bible provides examples of God Himself temporarily robbing men of their speech. In the Old Testament we see an example of this in the life of the prophet Ezekiel (Ezekiel 3:26; 24:27). We see God doing something similar in the life of Zacharias, the father of John the Baptist (Luke 1:19-22). Zacharias lost his speech because he failed to believe God's promise of a son. This is affirmed by the angel Gabriel when he said, "But behold, you will be mute and not able to speak until the day these things take place [John is born], because you did not believe my words" (Luke 1:20).

God's Provision for the Deaf

As in the case of blindness, we see God's protective hand on the deaf. The Lord says, "You shall not curse the deaf, nor put a stumbling block before the blind, but shall fear your God: I am the Lord" (Leviticus 19:14). Once again we see the Lord looking out for the helpless and defenseless. Surely the Lord loves and cares a great deal for the physically impaired—even to the point of creating special laws to protect these precious people.

Lameness

As we read through the Bible, we see various degrees of lameness mentioned. When the Bible refers to lameness in a literal sense, the condition ranges from a complete inability to walk to those who are partially hampered. When spoken of figuratively, lameness characterizes a fool's inability to appropriately share wisdom (Proverbs 26:7) and portrays spiritually weak Christians (Hebrews 12:12-13).

Lameness Brought on Naturally

During the early days of the church, we see an incident involving Peter and John (Acts 3:1-10). One day, while entering the temple at Jerusalem, a "man lame from his mother's womb" saw them and "asked for alms [money]" (Acts 3:2-3). Peter responded, "Silver and gold I do not have, but what I do have I give you" (Acts 3:6). Peter then healed the man of his lameness.

The passage gives us a brief glimpse of the sort of lameness that troubled the man when it says, "His feet and ankle bones received strength" (Acts 3:7). The passage does not indicate that any other portions of his body were impaired. Therefore we may assume he experienced some sort of paralysis limited to his feet and ankles. One thing is certain: the healing was miraculous and instantaneous. There appears to have been a number of people who knew the lame man prior to his healing (Acts 3:10). Thus, the man's lameness was verifiable. This adds to the credibility of the healing. (See Acts 14:8-10 for additional example.)

One of the most touching stories in Scripture surrounds Jonathan's five-year-old son, Mephibosheth. Upon hearing of the death of Jonathan and King Saul in battle, Mephibosheth's nurse "took him up and fled. And it happened, as she made haste to flee, that he fell and became lame" (2 Samuel 4:4). The boy's impairment was induced as a result of the nurse's flight. It appears when she dropped him, the boy's feet were crushed.

Years later King David honored a promise to show kindness to the members of Jonathan's family (1 Samuel 20:14-15, 16, 42). David gave Mephibosheth "all that belonged to Saul and to all his house" (2 Samuel 9:1-13). David also honored Jonathan by allowing Mephibosheth to eat at his "table like one of the king's sons" (2 Samuel 9:11).

David could easily have forgotten his promise to Jonathan, but he did not. As a true and loving friend, David exalted his deceased friend's son to the status of a prince and son. As sad as Mephibosheth's story is, because of David's graciousness, a happy ending was made possible for one who spent most of his life physically impaired.

Lameness Brought on Supernaturally

The closest example to lameness brought on supernaturally is seen in Genesis 32:24-31. There a man thought to be the angel of the Lord wrenched Jacob's hip in such a way as to cause him to walk with a limp.

Other Bodily Deficiencies

The Bible mentions Jesus healing the lame, but there is no indication of the impairment's origin (Matthew 11:5; 15:30-31; 21:14). Other examples of bodily loss include a withering or drying up of a body part (Lamentations 4:8; Mark 3:1; Luke 6:6), an impaired arm (Job 31:22; 38:15), a broken neck (1 Samuel 4:18), general deficiencies and deformities (Leviticus 21:18-19), and even a bad tooth (Proverbs 25:19).

Scripture also includes examples of those who have been maimed. This condition may occur as a result of accident, punishment, or ill will on the part of an adversary. It denotes those who have been severely injured or mutilated (Judges 1:6; Leviticus 21:18; Matthew 15:30; Mark 9:43; Luke 14:13).

Bodily Irregularities

The second category mentioned in the Bible is that of bodily irregularities. This is a broad class of impairments and afflictions characterized by some form of partial dysfunction. The severity varies from case to case.

Barrenness

In Scripture we see an irregularity that appears to have been present throughout the history of man. It is usually referred to as barrenness. When used literally, barrenness refers to women who are unable to bear children. At times it is clearly the result of God depriving a person of the ability to reproduce. In some cases it acts as a distinct sign of His disfavor (Leviticus 20:20-21). In other instances the Lord uses barrenness to help people recognize His sovereignty over particular situations and all things in general.

Barrenness is used figuratively to describe the terrain of a particular land mass (Job 39:6). Occasionally it was used to express the ground's inability to produce crops (2 Kings 2:19). It was also used to denote a spiritual lacking or deficiency due to an inferior relationship with Christ (2 Peter 1:8).

Barrenness Brought on Naturally

Psalm 127:3-5 says, "Children are a heritage from the Lord, the fruit of the womb is a reward." Even though the Bible strongly links childbearing with God's divine blessing, it would be unwise to assume that all barrenness is a product of supernatural intervention.

When examining the subject, little is said concerning non-induced barrenness. Yet the Bible does not go so far as to say all barrenness is a direct result of God's hand. It appears Scripture sees no need to address the obvious. Therefore, it seems safe to say most cases of barrenness are simply by-products of some sort of biological equalizer (Matthew 5:45) rather than an indicator of God's divine favor or disfavor upon a given person.

Barrenness Brought on Supernaturally

Interestingly enough, as we skim through the Bible, we see some of its most prominent women bearing a form of induced barrenness: Sarah (Genesis 11:30), Rebekah (Genesis 25:21), Rachel (Genesis 29:31), Manoah's wife (Judges 13:2-3), Hannah (1 Samuel 1:5), and Elisabeth (Luke 1:7). One might wonder why God caused each of these women to undergo a period of barrenness? Was it to punish them? To stigmatize them before their peers? There is no indication any of them were barren due to God's disfavor.

It appears God used their barrenness to solidify the reality of His presence in their lives and the lives of their children. Sarah and Rebekah eventually gave birth to Isaac and Jacob—two of the patriarchs (Genesis 18:10; 27:27-29). Rachel gave birth to Joseph, who was made the second most powerful man in all of Egypt by Pharaoh (Genesis 41:41-45). Manoah's wife gave birth to mighty Samson (Genesis 13:24). Hannah gave birth to the prophet Samuel (1 Samuel 1:20; 3:20). Elisabeth gave birth to John the Baptist (Luke 1:57). Clearly, God was not punishing these women and their husbands, but using their lives to demonstrate His presence and redemptive purpose through them and their offspring.

Because the Bible often associates barrenness with women, many are led to believe Scripture attributes such things only to women. This is not the case. The Bible recognizes this potential both in male and female. This becomes evident when God said to Israel, "You shall be blessed above all peoples; there shall not be a male or female barren among you" (Deuteronomy 7:14). The word barren indicates the essence of sterility. Notice the verse refers to both "male" and "female." Thus, in those places where the Bible attributes barrenness to women, it does so not because of some sort of hidden bias, but rather because God prophetically directed the writer in this manner.

Circumcision

A second bodily irregularity seen in the Bible is the practice of circumcision. The removal of the foreskin as seen in Scripture, began with God's covenant with Abraham (Genesis 17:9-14). The Lord used circumcision as a "sign of the covenant" (Genesis 17:11) between God and Abraham. It was to include all males belonging to the household of Abraham. Circumcision was to be practiced in all subsequent generations as God commanded Abraham, saying, "He who is eight days old among you shall be circumcised, every male child in your generations" (Genesis 17:12). Failure to maintain the practice was deemed as breaking God's covenant, and offenders were to be ostracized (Genesis 17:14). The sign of circumcision is practiced by the descendants of Abraham to this day.

Figuratively, uncircumcision was used to denote those who were spiritually unclean or incomplete in some way. Moses described himself as a man of "uncircumcised lips" (Exodus 6:30). The Lord referred to Israel as those whose "ear is uncircumcised" (Jeremiah 6:10). What initially began as an outward physical sign acknowledging God's covenant with Abraham eventually came to differentiate one's moral standing before God.

Other Bodily Irregularities

Beyond barrenness and circumcision, we see other bodily irregularities mentioned in the Bible on a less frequent scale. We see such things as stammering (Isaiah 32:4), baldness (Leviticus 13:40), feebleness (Psalm 38:8; Ezekiel 7:17), afflicted hip/joint (Genesis 32:25), uncontrollable trembling/shaking (Job 4:14; Jeremiah 23:9), forms of bodily uncleanness (Leviticus 12-15), and miscarriage (Exodus 21:22-23).

Bodily Ailments

The last major category of physical impairments seen in the Bible is that of bodily ailments. There are many different types of ailments mentioned in Scripture. Most of them may be considered either diseases or sicknesses, but because of the unusual nature of some, there is room for exception.

Skin Conditions

In both the Old and New Testaments we see the mention of leprosy and other skin conditions. Scripture provides examples of both non-induced and induced leprosy. By definition leprosy is "a slowly progressing and intractable disease characterized by subcutaneous nodules, scabs or cuticular crusts and white shining spots appearing to be deeper than the skin."[1] Because the language used to characterize leprosy in the Bible tends to be a vague and comprehensive terminology, it must not be confused with the modern notions of the disease.

Leprosy is first mentioned in reference to Moses. It occurred when Moses stood before the burning bush on Mount Horeb and God commanded him to go to Egypt to free captive Israel. Moses, being unsure of himself, said to God, "Suppose they will not believe me or listen to my voice; suppose they say, 'The Lord has not appeared to you.'" (Exodus 4:1). God responded by first turning Moses' staff into a snake, then causing his hand to become "leprous" (Exodus 4:3, 6). God used leprosy to convince Moses of His divine presence in this massive undertaking.

In the book of Leviticus, chapters 13 and 14 (also Numbers 5:2-4; Deuteronomy 24:8), we see detailed sections describing various infectious skin diseases and how the priests were to recognize and deal with them. These sections should not be considered to hold any modern diagnostic value.

Other instances of those developing skin conditions include Miriam's induced leprosy (Numbers 12:10); boils (Exodus 9:8-12); sores (Job 2:7); boils, tumors, the scab and the itch (Deuteronomy 28:27); Naaman (2 Kings 5:1); Gehazi (2 Kings 5:27); the lepers of Samaria (2 Kings 7:3); Uzziah (2 Kings 15:5); the ten lepers (Luke 17:12); and the leper Jesus touched (Matthew 8:2).

Palsy

Of the many bodily ailments seen in the Bible, palsy (a paralytic) is mentioned on several occasions. Palsy is "characterized by

---

1. S.B. Brown, "Leprosy," *The Wycliffe Bible Encyclopedia*, Volumn 2, p. 1026.

extreme loss of the power of motion dependent on some affection either of the motor centers of the brain or of the spinal cord."[2] (See Matthew 9:2; Luke 5:18; Acts 9:33.)

One of the most well-known depictions of a person afflicted with palsy is the account of the paralytic lowered through a roof (Luke 5:18-26). One day, while Jesus was busy teaching and healing the sick, men carrying a paralytic on a mat attempted to place him before Jesus that he might be healed. Because the crowd was so large, they were unable to do so. As a result, they went up on the roof and lowered the paralytic "through the tiles into the middle of the crowd, right in front of Jesus" (Luke 5).

This account helps us understand the desperateness of the sick in Jesus' day and the level of faith they had in His ability to heal. The men believed in Christ and were not going to be denied.

Within this account we also see the extreme conditions the sick had to endure. The paralytic's only means of transportation was a mat carried by some friends. He had no motorized wheelchair, no van with a special lift. To get around, he was completely dependent on the crude devices of others. This reminds us how blessed we are to live in an age where modern technology has helped the physically impaired overcome some of life's obstacles.

Stomach Infirmity

In his epistles, the apostle Paul sometimes used word pictures that allow us to peek into the world of his day. One such glimpse is when Paul wrote to his understudy, Timothy, saying, "No longer drink only water, but use a little wine for your stomach's sake and your frequent infirmities" (1 Timothy 5:23). Apparently, young Timothy must have told Paul of his numerous infirmities. This led the apostle to recommend a potential cure.

In this short account, we see Timothy regularly suffering from some sort of stomach ailment. This is not surprising, as such things were common then and remain so even today. One of the first things a tourist is told when visiting the Middle East is "Don't drink the water."

---

2. Alexander MacAlister, "Palsy," *The International Standard Bible Encyclopedia*, Volumn IV, p. 2236.

Paul, being a well-traveled man, realized the source of Timothy's ailment was the water. Accordingly, the apostle told the young pastor to "use a little wine." Paul believed a little wine would have a settling effect on the pastor's stomach. His advice must have been effective, for in 2 Timothy Paul's concern over the problem is no longer mentioned.

Other Bodily Ailments

The Bible provides a host of additional bodily ailments. We see in the thirty-ninth year of Asa's reign as king of Judah, he was "diseased in his feet" (1 Kings 15:23; 2 Chronicles 16:12). The nature of the disease is unknown. But it was severe enough that it eventually killed him. We also see that King Jehoram suffered from an induced disease of the intestines (2 Chronicles 21:15-19). The specifics of the disease are unknown, yet we know he suffered greatly from it over a two-year period. The disease ultimately caused his bowels to come out, which led to his death.

Other bodily ailments briefly mentioned are rottenness of bone (Habakkuk 3:16), induced abdominal swelling (Numbers 5:21), induced snake bite leading to death (Numbers 21:7), bleeding for twelve years (Luke 8:43), worms (Acts 12:23), fever and dysentery (Acts 28:8), dropsy (Luke 14:2), cancer (2 Timothy 2:17), inflammation and fever (Deuteronomy 28:22), and general wounds (Isaiah 1:6; Jeremiah 30:12; Nahum 3:19).

Mental Impairment

Some may wonder if the Bible recognizes the presence of mental impairments. Although Scripture does not say much regarding this, it does refer to it in several places.

One of the most well-known examples is seen in the life of David. In 1 Samuel 21:10-15 David pretended to be insane, as he feared Achish King of Gath.

This passage is important in that it acknowledges the presence of insanity. Both David and Achish recognized various instances of mental impairments within their societies. Apparently insanity was so widespread within Gath it caused Achish to say to his men, "Have I need of madmen, that you have brought this fellow to play the madman in my presence?" Clearly, the mentally impaired were nothing new to Gath (See Deuteronomy 28:28 and Proverbs 26:18.)

God-Induced Insanity

In Daniel 4 we see an example of God-induced insanity directed at Nebuchadnezzar, king of Babylon. God used this impairment to punish Nebuchadnezzar because he took credit for his success as king rather than crediting God for it (Daniel 4:30). The insanity took the form of lycanthropy—man viewing himself as an animal and living like one.

Other Mention of Mental Impairment

In both Matthew 4:24 and 17:15 we see examples of epilepsy. The descriptions and details given in both cases are limited.

As we conclude, it is important to remember this section is not exhaustive, but rather a brief survey of most of the impairments and afflictions mentioned in the Bible. Much more could be shared, but that is not our purpose. Our goal has been to observe the sort of impairments contained in the Bible and provide a sampling of the context surrounding them.

Keep in mind, Scripture did not have to mention even one impairment, yet it mentions many. When God's Word was written, the Lord could have conveniently swept the blind, the deaf, the dumb, the barren, the sick and diseased under the rug. But He did not attempt to hide such things; rather, He featured them in some cases. Why? Because the Bible and the lives included in it are real. Scripture depicts a real God, dealing with real people who obtain real impairments.

In God's plan, such things won't last forever. One day all those in Christ will be made anew. What does that mean? No more pain. No more suffering. And of course, no more physical impairments or afflictions.

5 The Agony of Victory

The plight of the physically impaired is an ongoing reality. The pain, trials, and social stigmatism accompanied by some impairments make them a formidable challenge.

Thankfully, the travail of the impaired is temporary. When a person dies, the impairment no longer maintains its powerful grip on the afflicted. Consequently, for some, death is not a curse, but a blessing—it is not a source of bondage, but freedom!

Spiritual Impairment

Many who are suffering, or care for someone who is suffering, look at death as the ultimate means of dealing with such afflictions. Some view death as an end, rather than a beginning. They see it as a cure, not a plague. The Bible teaches death is man's enemy, not his friend (1 Corinthians 15:26; 2 Corinthians 1:9; 4:12). Psalm 49:14 says, "Like sheep they are laid in the grave; Death shall feed on them."

Death does not liberate man—it feeds on him. Death is a spiritual affliction, just as disease is a physical one.

Romans 5:12 says of death, "Therefore, just as through one man sin entered the world, and death through sin, and thus death spread to all men, because all sinned." Death is a by-product of man's sin. Through Adam, the corrupting effects of sin have permeated the heart and soul of all men—"for all have sinned and fall short of the glory of God" (Romans 3:23).

As much suffering as physical affliction may bring, it pales in comparison to the far-reaching effects of spiritual impairment. Murder, sex crimes, drug addiction, racism, abortion, war, poverty, physical impairments and the like, find their source in man's spiritual impairment.

Unlike the transitory nature of the physical body, man's immaterial soul exists forever. Thus, spiritual impairment survives the grave to afflict its host eternally. The Bible says the ultimate consequence of this impairment is spiritual death and eternal separation from God in a place of torment known as the *lake of fire* (Romans 6:23; Revelation 20:15).

The Bible teaches that sin is an active choice of the human will. Therefore, we may conclude that man is not robotically programmed to sin. As a result, all men are rightly held accountable, judged and punished by God for sins committed in this life.

Jesus said, "Whoever looks at a woman to lust for her has already committed adultery with her in his heart" (Matthew 5:28). Later He added, "But I say to you that for every idle word men may speak, they will give account of it in the day of judgment" (Matthew 12:36). Without question, God's standards of judgment are very high.

God holds us accountable for what we say, what we think, and even our motives. With this sort of standard, who is free from sin? Who can possibly escape God's judgment? The Bible says that no one will be spared based on the good they have done, for "We are all like an unclean thing, and all our righteousnesses are like filthy rags; we all fade as a leaf, and our iniquities, like the wind, have taken us away" (Isaiah 64:6; see also Ephesians 2:8-9).

If this is the case, why would anyone view death as a source of freedom? Apart from spiritual healing, death cannot be associated with liberation.

Spiritual Healing

Almost instinctively, when people are severely injured or ill, they seek the help of a qualified physician. They realize their problem is beyond their ability to manage, and apart from a doctor the outcome is uncertain.

When I injured my foot, if I had ignored the seriousness of the injury, the bones would have set in a manner that would have distorted my heel. By allowing a physician to treat my injury, I am able to walk normal today. Why? Because through a physician's expert care, I found healing.

I find it interesting that most people are quick to grasp the need for medical intervention when it comes to matters of physical health, but are oblivious to the need for intervention when it comes to spiritual matters. When hurting physically, we go to a physician. When hurting spiritually, we suppress the need. Why ignore the obvious? Address the spiritual impairment as you would the physical.

Some might see this suggestion as ridiculous, but the Bible speaks of the true Physician who specializes in spiritual healing. The name of the doctor is Jesus Christ. He said, "Those who are well have no need of a physician, but those who are sick. I have not come to call the righteous, but sinners, to repentance" (Luke 5:31-32). The Lord used the analogy of a medical doctor to help establish man's spiritual need. He affirmed man's sin sickness and informed us of His willingness to treat those afflicted by it.

The Physician's Prescription

Like those suffering from a unique physical affliction, the spiritually impaired can only find healing through a precise treatment. Knowing this, the Lord came into the world for the purpose of providing the only prescription capable of overcoming spiritual impairment. He did so in order to make it available to men.

There are three elements in Christ's prescription.

His Affliction

The first element of Jesus' prescription was His personal affliction. The culmination of the Lord's purpose here on earth began with His suffering. The suffering He experienced was mental, emotional, physical, and even spiritual in nature.

Mental Suffering

Throughout the Lord's earthly ministry, we see indications that He knew one day He would suffer on behalf of sinful man (Matthew 16:21; 20:17-19). Surely, possessing knowledge of any type of suffering is trying, but harboring things such as the betrayal,

Peter's denial, the cross, and all that surrounded it must have been extremely difficult to bear.

The Lord, maintaining godly discipline over His thought life, refused to allow such things to rule over Him. Yet when reproving Peter for his "rebuke" (Matthew 16:22), Jesus was quick to point out that Peter's words were as a mental "stumbling block" to Him. Jesus likened Peter's words to those of the devil, saying, "Get behind Me, Satan" (Matthew 16:23).

The quickness and sharpness of Christ's rebuke gives us a glimpse of the mental struggle He faced when encountering such trials. The last thought He wanted to entertain was that of denying His Father's will. As a result, Jesus slapped Peter with the strongest of rebukes. In doing so, He fought and won the battle of the heart and mind. His ability to overcome this obstacle is reminiscent of an earlier encounter He had with the devil (Luke 4:1-12).

Emotional Suffering

We realize the depth of Christ's emotional suffering as we observe His actions just prior to His betrayal while at the Mount of Olives. There we see Him crying out to God the Father, saying, "Father, if it is Your will, take this cup away from Me" (Luke 22:42). The cup Jesus was referring to was the physical and spiritual suffering He would soon partake of.

Like any emotionally sound person, Christ suffered inwardly over the torture that would soon take place. The Bible says He was in "agony" even to the point that "His sweat became like great drops of blood" (Luke 22:44). Unquestionably, this is a description of a man who was undergoing severe emotional trauma and suffering.

Physical Suffering

Jesus not only had to deal with mental and emotional anguish, but with physical suffering as well. After Christ was arrested, He was treated terribly. He was repeatedly slapped, beaten, and whipped until His back was a bloody pulp.

After the physical torture leading up to the crucifixion, one would think Jesus had suffered enough. But for those who despised Him, it wasn't! The religious leaders would not be satisfied until Christ was dead. Thus, they demanded His crucifixion.

The Lord's crucifixion involved the driving of three rusty and jagged spikes into His hands and feet. Once that was accomplished, Jesus was set upright on the cross to begin the final stage of this torturous suffering.

In his article titled "The Crucifixion of Jesus, The Passion of Christ from a Medical Point of View," Dr. C. Truman Davis gives us an idea of the level of Christ's physical pain. He says that Jesus' suffering consisted of "limitless pain, cycles of twisting, joint-rending cramps, intermittent partial asphyxiation, searing pain as tissue is torn from His lacerated back as He moves up and down against the rough timber." This was followed by "crushing pain deep in the chest as the pericardium slowly fills with serum and begins to compress the heart."[1]

As we consider Dr. Davis's description of Christ's physical suffering, we realize the agony He experienced on our behalf is beyond comprehension.

Spiritual Suffering

As terrible as the mental, emotional, and physical suffering must have been, the greatest torture Christ experienced seems to have been spiritual in nature. Throughout Christ's trials and anguish, Scripture presents only one instance of distress on His part.

At one point during the crucifixion, it appears Jesus experienced a momentary crisis. What brought it on? Was it the humiliating circumstances He was forced to endure? Was it the unyielding pain He had suffered? Perhaps it was the thought of impending death that shook Him. As difficult as each of these things were, Jesus seemed to weather them in an exceptional manner. Rather, the breakdown is revealed in the question, "My God, My God, why have You forsaken Me?" (Matthew 27:46).

The Bible says when Jesus spoke these words, He "cried out with a loud voice" (Matthew 27:46). From the moment of the first cruel slap up to the point of His death, Scripture indicates the Lord "cried" out only twice. The first we already mentioned; the second occurred when He gave up His spirit.

What was it that caused Jesus to cry out, "My God, My God, why have You forsaken Me?" Christ cried out because He felt the desperation of suffering brought on by spiritual separation from His Father. Imagine a life of unbroken fellowship with God the Father from cradle to cross, and the absolute agony and abandonment a person would feel if broken.

---

1. C.T. Davis, The Crucifixion of Jesus (Arizona: Arizona Medicine, 1965)

We get a small taste of this special bond when Christ says, "No one knows the Son except the Father, and no one knows the Father except the Son and those to whom the Son chooses to reveal Him" (Matthew 11:27). The word *knows* goes beyond the concept of mere recognition or acknowledgment. Rather, here it is meant to characterize a relationship permeated with inexpressible love and intimacy between the two parties. When such a relationship is broken, even momentarily, anguish surpassing even the torture of the cross is immediately realized. Thus, in a naked outburst of raw emotions, like a child being torn from the bosom of its mother, Jesus cried out, "My God, My God, why have You forsaken Me?"

Truly, of all the suffering Jesus experienced—mental, emotional, and physical—none could compare with the anguish He felt when forsaken by His Father.

His Death

The second element in the Lord's prescription was His death. Even though Christ endured a great deal of humiliation and suffering to pay the price for man's sin, in and of itself, that was not enough.

Because of the degree of man's wrong, he rightly deserved the sentence of death. As a result, when Christ took man's sin upon Himself, the death sentence naturally accompanied it (2 Corinthians 5:18-21).

The shedding of blood and sacrificial death Christ experienced were foreshadowed by the Old Testament sacrificial system established by God (Leviticus 1:1-17; 4:1-5, 19; 7:1-7, 16). It taught that sin is so offensive to God, the only way to effectively resolve cases involving it was through the sacrifice of a designated male animal bearing no defect. The sacrifice was meant to represent the shedding of innocent blood on behalf of sinful man. Indeed, Jesus Himself was without the defect of sin; thus He was the only one capable of fulfilling this essential requirement established by the Father.

The apostle Paul explained the purpose of Christ's sacrificial death in Romans 3:25-26, saying:

> God set forth as a propitiation [covering over sin in such a way as to make reconciliation between God and man], by His [Jesus] blood, through faith, to demonstrate His righteousness, because in His forbearance God had passed over the sins that

were previously committed, to demonstrate at the present time His righteousness, that He might be just and the justifier of the one who has faith in Jesus.

Christ's death was essential in that without it there would be no payment for man's sin. And with no payment, there would be no hope of reconciliation between God and man, for sin would act as an impenetrable barrier between the two. With this in mind, it becomes easy to understand why Jesus' death was an essential part of His prescription.

His Resurrection

The final aspect to Christ's prescription was His resurrection from the dead. Why was this an essential element in His prescription for treating the spiritually impaired? Because Jesus' resurrection verified the reality of His claim to be the Son of God. If Christ had not risen from the dead, He would have proved Himself to be a fool and a liar—a fool in that He would have died needlessly, and a liar because He promised the world He would rise from the dead on the third day (Luke 18:33).

By rising from the dead, Jesus overcame sin and death. If He had not risen from the dead, both sin and death would continue to reign supreme over all men.

The Treatment's Result

Christ's affliction, death, and resurrection form a powerful medicine for overcoming spiritual impairments resulting from sin. Scripture says because of the Great Physician's prescription, all who truly partake of it shall be cured of this spiritual affliction.

How does one partake of this holy remedy? It all begins by recognizing the problem. Like any affliction, treatment seems unnecessary until the need becomes evident. In this case, sin is the problem, but until we see it for what it is, Christ's cure will spark no urgency and thereby appear irrelevant.

To help us acknowledge the importance of the Physician's prescription, the Bible says, "All have sinned and fall short of the glory of God" (Romans 3:23). The word *all* indicates that everyone, without exception, has a sin problem that has created this spiritual impairment.

Just as a physical impairment may overshadow and disallow certain vital activities, spiritual impairment does the same in that it completely nullifies any possibility of a true relationship with God. But by recognizing our sin problem, confessing it to God, and by faith actively turning from sin to Christ and His cure, spiritual healing through salvation is ours.

This is important because anyone can recognize a problem, and perhaps even a remedy, but until we faithfully partake of it, it can have no positive influence on us. Similarly, as we fully embrace the Lord's suffering, death, and resurrection from the dead, we can joyously proclaim with the apostle Paul:

> Death is swallowed up in victory. O Death, where is your sting? O Hades, where is your victory? The sting of death is sin, and the strength of sin is the law. But thanks be to God, who gives us the victory through our Lord Jesus Christ. (1 Corinthians 15:54-57)

The Physician's Victory

The Physician's agony resulted in His victory over sin and death once and for all. The product of His victory contains many great and wonderful benefits for those who claim it as their own.

Spiritual Healing and Life

Those who partake of Christ's remedy are guaranteed healing from spiritual impairment. Where once the prognosis was certain death, through the healing ministry of the Great Physician there is life eternal. (See Galatians 6:8; 1 John 5:13.)

Spiritual Victory

Apart from God's intervention, man faces a life of spiritual defeat. Like a one-legged runner racing in the Olympics, the spiritually handicapped, no matter how sincere or how great their effort, are destined to lose. The good news is, because of God's gracious healing and new life, spiritual victory is free to those wishing to partake of His holy prescription.

Men are no longer held captive to the failure associated with sin, but may claim victory through Christ. The apostle John said, "For whatever is born of God overcomes the world. And this is the victory that has overcome the world—our faith" (1 John 5:4).

Many people spend their lives striving to become spiritually successful. They may perform all sorts of acts of "goodness" in an attempt to earn spiritual victory. But as the apostle said, only those "born of God" through "faith" can gain eternal success.

Those outside of Christ are equipped for spiritual failure. The only way to gain the Lord's victory is on His terms. His victory is a free gift and all one must do is trust in Him as Lord and Savior.

Spiritual Relationships

Man was once estranged from God and His spiritual offspring, but through Christ's sacrifice, a true relationship with Him and His church becomes a reality. Those who find spiritual healing in Christ become sons and daughters, joint heirs with Him for all eternity. Paul said, "The Spirit Himself bears witness with our spirit that we are children of God, and if children, then heirs—heirs of God and joint heirs with Christ, if indeed we suffer with Him, that we may also be glorified together" (Romans 8:16-17).

At the time of salvation, those who become children of God are baptized and sealed by the Holy Spirit, making their godly union irreversible. The Holy Spirit then works to instruct and guide believers in the ways of God through the Bible, prayer, preaching, teaching and the like.

Spiritual Residence

Christ the risen victor said, "In My Father's house are many mansions; if it were not so, I would have told you. I go to prepare a place for you. And if I go and prepare a place for you, I will come again and receive you to Myself; that where I am, there you may be also" (John 14:2-3). When the Lord ascended to heaven, He did so for a purpose: to prepare a place for His followers.

This is a wonderful thought. Even now Jesus is preparing a spiritual residence for His people. Unlike our earthly dwellings, the place He prepares has no strings attached—no rental or mortgage payments, no fire, floods, or storms to destroy it. The place He prepares is magnificent and made to last forever.

For those who have found spiritual healing in Christ, there is much to look forward to. Darkness has been turned to light. The night is dawning into a new day.

Physically Impaired, Yet Spiritually Healthy

The plight of the physically impaired is temporary, not eternal, so for some death is not a curse, but a blessing. Death is not a source of bondage, but freedom. How is this possible? Through the miraculous healing power of Jesus Christ.

There are many things in life the physically impaired cannot do because of their afflictions; obtaining spiritual healing is not one of them. A person can be physically impaired, yet find spiritual health through the Lord.

After a person rids himself of his spiritual impairment, death need not be looked upon as a curse or a source of bondage anymore, for in God's appointed time, death helps us shed the bondage of our frail and mortal bodies. Thus, like Paul, we too can say, "For to me, to live is Christ, and to die is gain" (Philippians 1:21).

All those in Christ are meant to faithfully serve God until He calls them home. When that time comes, all true followers of Christ bearing physical impairments will be made free and whole. The Lord will grant each one an unimpaired heavenly body, one that will never suffer decay—a glorious body that will never see injury or illness again.

Scripture says, "For our citizenship is in heaven, from which we also eagerly wait for the Savior, the Lord Jesus Christ, who will transform our lowly body that it may be conformed to His glorious body" (Philippians 3:20-21). The body spoken of here will be a resurrection body, magnificent in nature—a precious gift of God.

The Lord's gracious gift of spiritual healing is available to all, whether they be physically impaired or not. Jesus suffered the greatest impairment of all to provide us with victory through His salvation. As a result, the great Physician's remedy is free for everyone desiring to partake of it.

6 The Calling

A favorite pastime for many is checking out the sights and sounds of a vintage antique car show. People are transported back to yesteryear when in the presence of these time machines on wheels.

On several occasions my father-in-law and I had the pleasure of attending a show together. Because he's relatively knowledgeable about some of the earlier models, he'll often provide a little background regarding a vehicle's history.

An added dimension to attending such a show with someone like him is that he is able to point out various adaptations that were not part of the original cars. The modern colors, modified engines, and neat little gadgets all remind us that in one sense the old car is still there, yet in another sense we're observing something unique and new.

Those who have found spiritual healing through Jesus Christ are like those antique cars. In one sense the "old" person remains, but as a result of Christ's transforming power, they have become something unique and new as well.

Upon acceptance of Jesus as Savior, we immediately become new creatures. The Bible says, "Therefore, if anyone is in Christ, he is a new creation; old things have passed away; behold, all things have become new" (2 Corinthians 5:17). Because of Christ's sacrificial death, true followers are no longer viewed by God as sinners, but as saints. Through Christ, our old life has been put behind us, and our new one graciously placed before us.

Within this new life, all believers are called to become more like Jesus. The apostle John made this clear when he said, "Everyone who has this hope in Him purifies himself, just as He is pure" (1 John 3:3). Becoming more like Jesus is the goal Christ's followers are given at the point of salvation, and strive to attain throughout their earthly lives.

When referring to the Christian's calling, the apostle Paul said:

> Put off, concerning your former conduct, the old man which grows corrupt according to the deceitful lusts, and be renewed in the spirit of your mind, and that you put on the new man which was created according to God, in true righteousness and holiness. (Ephesians 4:22-24)

Paul said, that becoming more like Christ entails putting off the "old man" and putting on the "new."

Putting Off

Prior to his fall, Adam was perfect in every way. When he chose sin over a relationship with God, Adam and his wife became spiritually impaired. Christ came into the world to provide a remedy for man's spiritual woes. Those who partake of His holy treatment, receive new life and spiritual healing. One of the key elements of embracing that new life is putting off the old life, along with all the excess baggage that accompanies it.

Paul said, "Put off . . . the old man." Putting off the old man (or self) is like regaining the use of a badly damaged limb. Regardless of how badly a person wants to be healed, it is a slow and orderly process. As with the physical, spiritual healing demands a slow and orderly process.

Far too often new Christians are not afforded the opportunity to move from spiritual immaturity to maturity in an orderly manner. This sets them up for needless frustration and failure.

Spiritual Surgery

When I broke my heel the doctor took X-rays to determine the problem. Once it was identified, I underwent corrective surgery. During the operation the surgeon carefully reconstructed my heel, fastening it together with six pins. He completed the procedure by securing a small metal plate to the side of my foot to reinforce a damaged joint. After three months of healing, I slowly began to engage in specialized physical therapy. Today I walk with a slight limp, but praise the Lord I am walking and continue to make positive strides.

As with my injury, before the spiritually impaired can think about recovery, they must identify their sin problem and allow the Great Physician to probe and perform spiritual surgery on their sin-sick heart. Only after this has been accomplished can true healing begin.

Sadly, many people today put the cart before the horse by engaging in a form of "spiritual therapy" even though they have never undergone the necessary spiritual surgery. Think of the damage I would have caused my heel if I had skipped surgery and immediately began physical therapy. Most would consider such a decision absurd, but this happens all the time when it comes to spiritual development.

People look to false religions, cults, and earning God's favor in an attempt to "therapeutically" heal the soul and gain salvation. But just as I needed specialized surgery and therapy for my injury, the spiritually impaired need Christ's remedy.

Some say there are many ways to find God and spiritual healing. But just as there was only one way to properly correct my physical impairment, there is only one way to truly correct man's spiritual impairment. Before we strive to "run" spiritually, we must learn to walk. Before we can do great things for God, we must first truly know Him and obtain healing through the great Physician.

Spiritual Therapy

In concert with Christ's surgical process, He also prescribes spiritual therapy for the heart and mind. One important aspect of His therapy is "putting off the old self."

The old self is a nature inclined to sin. All men are born with such a nature. Scripture says, "Those who live according to the flesh [sinful nature - NIV] set their minds on the things of the flesh" (Romans 8:5). Because of the desires of the old self, man by nature is prone to sin rather than pursue God's righteousness. Once this complication has been corrected, man is no longer bound by a sin nature. He is free to partake in a true relationship with God.

When Paul said, "Put off . . . the old man," it was as if he were saying, "Because you now have a spiritual relationship with God, you must likewise engage in spiritual therapy." In essence, "Christian, start working out all the debilitating effects of your past affliction."

The ingredients that formulate the old man may vary from person to person, but the fuel that fires its desires and activities is always the same: sin. Paul identified some of the potential activities the old self may encourage when he said:

> Now the works of the flesh are evident, which are: adultery, fornication, uncleanness, lewdness, idolatry, sorcery, hatred, contentions, jealousies, outbursts of wrath, selfish ambitions, dissensions, heresies, envy, murders, drunkenness, revelries, and the like. (Galatians 5:19-21)

Sinning involves an active choice of the will; putting off the old self does as well. Therefore, when Paul said, "Put off . . . the old man," he might well have said, "If prior to surrendering your life to Christ you were a sexually immoral person, now that you have entered into a true relationship with Him, commit yourself to ridding your life of the sexual immorality that has dominated you. If you were a jealous person, put off jealousy. If you were a drunk, put off drunkenness."

There is nothing mystical about the process. Paul is simply saying, "Now that you possess the ability through Christ to rid yourself of the sins that once ruled you, lay them aside." In striving to understand the process, we might think in terms of removing a nasty old coat. Once bathed and cleansed by the blood of Christ, make certain the old coat is removed and refuse to put it on. It's absurd to clothe one's self with filthy, vile garments after bathing.

In one sense, through Christ the disrobing takes place immediately. In another, the process of removing the old "coat" takes place one button at a time. It involves a consistent and ongoing effort.

Sadly, at times we may find ourselves re-buttoning a button we have already loosened. Nevertheless, all true followers of Christ are called to make active and daily strides toward putting off the old self.

If we find ourselves failing to make headway or we are consistently engaging in sins of the past, we must be willing to recognize the severity of our problem. For some, this may mean searching out the root cause, confessing all to Christ, seeking the Lord's forgiveness, and recommitting ourselves through the empowering of the Holy Spirit to follow Christ on His terms. For others, it may involve reexamining the reality of our relationship with Him.

There are some who, after reexamining their relationship, realize that they never truly accepted Jesus Christ as their Savior. If this is the case, earnestly go to Him in prayer, confessing your sin and acknowledge with both heart and mind your need for His loving grace, forgiveness, shed blood on the cross, and resurrection from the dead (Romans 3:23-26; 5:6-11; 6:23; 10:9-11; Ephesians 2:8-10).

We do so not because of feelings of insecurity or inferiority, but because we now realize that apart from Him, we are hopelessly lost and captives to sin. Thus, we are led to turn to our only hope and invite Him to reign in our hearts and direct our lives as our personal Lord and Savior. Only then will we truly begin to put off the old self and initiate the spiritual therapy and healing He offers.

Putting On

The believer in Christ is not only called to "put off . . . the old man," but to "put on the new man." Putting off the old self maintains the sense of ridding ourselves of that which is harmful to us. Putting on the "new man" involves the ongoing process of clothing ourselves with God's "righteousness and holiness" (Ephesians 4:24).

Put on Christ

What are some of the things Christians are called to "put on"? The first and most important is to "put on [or clothe ourselves with] the Lord Jesus Christ" (Romans 13:14; Galatians 3:27). What does that mean? Are we expected to wear Jesus like a coat? In a sense, yes. When covered with a coat, our body is completely encased in it. It surrounds us in such a way that it becomes part of us. It protects us and warms us from harmful elements. By putting on or clothing our hearts, minds, speech and senses with Christ, we're covered from the sinful elements of this world.

Why must we "put on" Christ? Because He is the Son of God (Romans 1:4), He first loved us (1 John 4:19), He suffered and died on our behalf (Acts 26:23), He is the "firstborn from the dead" (Revelation 1:5), He is the "head of the church" (Ephesians 5:23), and much more.

Why should we "put on" Christ? Because unlike all others, He has proven Himself to be a worthy "coat" for the believer. By identifying with Him, His life, and His teaching, we are dressed in a manner that no earthly apparel can match. As the hymn says, "Jesus shines brighter, Jesus shines purer, than all the angels heav'n can boast."[1]

Put on the Breastplate

As we robe ourselves with Jesus, the Word of God instructs us to "be sober [self-controlled], putting on the breastplate of faith and love" (1 Thessalonians 5:8). A breastplate is an armor plate that covers and protects vital body parts such as the heart. Those equipped with a breastplate during battle maintained a distinct advantage over those without one.

We are told to attire ourselves with faith and love in such a way that they act as a breastplate. The breastplate implies a sense of covering or guarding one's heart with these protective elements. In doing so, the Christian warrior is suited to ward off the many evils seeking to overtake the heart.

---

1. Munster Gesangbuch, "Fairest Lord Jesus," *Great Hymns of the Faith*, p. 50.

➤ Faith

The first element of the spiritual breastplate is faith. Why is faith important? Because it is the key to true salvation and a genuine relationship with God (Romans 3:25-26; 5:1).

The Bible says, "Without faith it is impossible to please Him, for he who comes to God must believe that He is" (Hebrews 11:6). There are those who say it doesn't matter what you believe as long as you believe. The God of the Bible does not agree with that assessment. Without true faith in God, Scripture says you cannot have a relationship with Him.

Is God's demand unfair? I don't believe so. The essence of faith in God is complete trust in Him. Even on a human level, how far can a relationship go if trust does not exist? Even thieves demand a level of trust between one another. And if thieves long for trustworthy relationships, is it wrong for God to expect anything less? Of course not.

It is essential that we "put on" true faith because Scripture says, "The just shall live by faith" (Romans 1:17). The life of the believer is characterized by faith (trust in God). Faith is necessary because man's understanding is limited to the small and momentary realities of life, whereas God is not. Man may be able to read other men's lips, but God can read their hearts (Acts 15:8). God, the Creator and Sustainer of the universe, can be trusted. He has never failed to uphold His word to man, whereas man has continually failed Him.

Through faith the believer in Christ can maintain a consistent and enduring walk with God. The Bible says, "We have dominion over your faith, but are fellow workers for your joy; for by faith you stand" (2 Corinthians 1:24). Surely it is not difficult to see why true faith is so important. Therefore, let us seek to clothe ourselves in a faith that is pleasing to God.

➤ Love

The second aspect of the spiritual breastplate is love. If faith is the key to salvation, love is that which prospers it. Christ-centered love not only prospers the salvation experience, it prospers everything that is righteous and good. Paul helps us grasp the importance of love by saying:

> Though I speak with the tongues of men and of angels, but have not love, I have become sounding brass or a clanging cymbal. And though I have the gift of prophecy, and understand all mysteries and all knowledge, and though I have all faith, so that I could remove mountains, but have not love, I am nothing. And though I bestow all my goods to feed the poor, and though I give my body to be burned, but have not love, it profits me nothing. (1 Corinthians 13:1-3)

Humanly speaking, if a person maintained all of these qualities with the exception of love, most people would consider that person to be great. The Bible on the other hand refers to such a person as being "nothing." How is that possible? God's ways are not man's ways. Man is impressed by outward signs—God is impressed with an inward reality that makes its way outward. To man, if it looks like love, it is. To God, anything short of true love is a recognizable counterfeit.

Put on God's Armor

Scripture says, "Put on the whole armor of God," which consists of truth, righteousness, the gospel of peace, faith, salvation, the Word of God, and praying in the Spirit (Ephesians 6:11-18; Romans 13:12).

What is the point of arraying ourselves with the armor? Again, it helps prepare us for spiritual warfare, it helps us maintain spiritual purity in the face of life's battles, and it guides us to certain victory over Satan and his evil forces.

For those who believe Satan is not interested in our downfall, listen to the words of the apostle Peter: "Be sober, be vigilant; because your adversary the devil walks about like a roaring lion, seeking whom he may devour" (1 Peter 5:8). Here Peter refers to Satan as our "adversary." In other words, he has no love for us—only hatred. He does not seek our betterment—only our downfall. Like a roaring lion, he looks not to feed us, but to feed on us.

In the first two chapters of the book of Job, we read of Satan "going to and fro on the earth, and from walking back and forth on it" seeking someone to devour. Believing he had a tasty morsel in Job, he viciously attacked the saint from every angle. But Job, fit for spiritual battle, overcame the evil one.

If we are going to succeed like Job, we too must be prepared for spiritual battle. The Lord provides everything necessary for our victory, but if we fail to dress in His armor, we have no one to blame but ourselves. Therefore, let us don truth, righteousness, the gospel of peace, faith, salvation, the Word of God, and prayer so that we too may embrace the victory.

Put on a Virtuous Demeanor

The attitude and actions of a Christian are important; thus, the Bible encourages us to "put on" a virtuous demeanor. Paul says, "Put on tender mercies, kindness, humility, meekness, longsuffering [patience]" (Colossians 3:12).

Virtues such as these help create an environment in which true fellowship is possible. In what way? By placing the lives of others higher than our own. These traits help us fulfill the second greatest commandment which is to "love your neighbor as yourself" (Leviticus 19:18). Showing genuine care and concern for others goes a long way toward building bridges. Inconsiderateness, meanness, pride, roughness criticalness, and wrongful intolerance all work to destroy relationships.

The sort of children we raise, the type of people we are, the kind of churches we attend, and the society we live in depend a great deal on the way we view virtuosity. By our actions, we can encourage compassion or indifference, kindness or cruelty, humility or haughtiness, gentleness or harshness, patience or anxiousness—the choice is ours. To build or not to build, that is our choice.

For those who are true disciples of Christ, a virtuous demeanor is not an option. We are called to "put on" things such as this. Thus, strengthening and building up others is simply a normal part of the Christian life.

➤Preparation

Putting off the old self and putting on the new does not come without its share of work. As people come to know Christ, in most cases they come with little knowledge of the Lord and His teachings. Therefore, we must spend time in preparation.

The process of preparation is lifelong and daily in nature. Because no one (in this life) ever truly masters the ways of Christ, spiritual *therapy* never ceases. On the contrary, Christians tend to climb from one level of spiritual maturity to another.

In order to better understand the necessity of personal preparation, there are three fundamental aspects we must consider.

➤Learn God's Word

It is impossible to grow and develop as a Christian apart from learning God's Word. In our quest to put off the old self and put on the new, apart from the Bible, how are we to discern between appropriate and inappropriate behavior? Apart from godly instruction, we will either fail to progress or our progression will be slow and sporadic, bearing little meaning.

The Bible says, "All Scripture is given by inspiration of God, and is profitable for doctrine, for reproof, for correction, for instruction in righteousness, that the man of God may be complete, thoroughly equipped for every good work" (2 Timothy 3:16-17). This passage alerts us to the ever-present wealth, usefulness, and wellspring of growth the Word of God provides both the novice and mature in Christ. Most assuredly, the Bible contains everything necessary for faith and practice. Therefore, everyone who seriously desires to develop in their walk will drink from the Bible daily and approach His Word with zeal.

➤Live God's Word

Learning God's Word is very important. But there is a difference between raw intellect and godly wisdom. Many people, down through the ages, have possessed incredible sums of head knowledge about Scripture, but they failed to obtain a true heart knowledge of it. One good example of this is the lives of the chief priests and elders who orchestrated Christ's crucifixion. These men knew the Old Testament Scriptures very well, yet their brilliance did not turn them to God; rather it turned them away from Him. Many liberal theologians have advanced degrees and have even written books on various aspects of the Bible, yet deny its authority.

Learning God's Word is very important, but embracing and living it is of greater importance. As we learn from it, the reality and depth of our faith is evidenced by the changes it brings to our lives.

In a moving and poetic fashion the psalmist said, "Your statutes have been my songs in the house of my pilgrimage. I remember Your name in the night, O Lord, and I keep Your law" (Psalm 119:54-55). Wherever the psalmist went, day or night, in word and in song, God's Word was an active part of his life. The psalmist loved Scripture so much it found expression in every aspect of his life.

Later the psalmist established the vital link between learning and living by saying, "The righteousness of Your testimonies is everlasting; Give me understanding, and I shall live" (Psalm 119:144). To the psalmist, understanding and life were inseparable. God's Word is seen as the only pattern for godly living, the only means of preserving life, and the true path to eternal life.

Those who have tasted of the fruit of Christ's salvation can agree with the psalmist. Jesus said, "I have come that they may have life, and that they may have it more abundantly" (John 10:10). The Lord said He came to offer the fullness of life. As we partake of His Word and apply it to our lives, the riches of this fullness will make its presence known.

➤Lend God's Word

As the believer begins to grasp the teachings and the practical relevance of Scripture, the natural desire to lend (or share) God's Word with others begins to surface—for some the desire is immediate. Soon after Philip followed the call of Christ, he found Nathanael and told him, "We have found Him of whom Moses in the law, and also the prophets, wrote—Jesus of Nazareth, the son of Joseph" (John 1:45). Once Philip believed, he could not contain this news. In haste he found another to share the good news with.

Regardless of how soon one begins to share Jesus with others, it is something all true believers are meant to take part in. The Bible says, "If you confess with your mouth the Lord Jesus and believe in your heart that God has raised Him from the dead, you will be saved" (Romans 10:9). Notice how closely Scripture links sharing news of Christ with that of possessing salvation.

We are not literally saved by sharing Christ with others, for salvation comes by faith alone (Ephesians 2:8). Rather, our confession is an outward sign of an inward reality. As we confess the Lord Jesus to others and share all He has done for us, we affirm before God and man the reality of our relationship with Him.

How does confession affirm our personal faith and trust in Christ? Simply put, would someone worshipping Allah refer to Jesus as Lord God? What about a follower of Buddha? Neither would because they have not accepted Jesus as Lord and Savior. Therefore, their silence in contrast to the believer's confession, speaks volumes as to the substance of their faith.

If we truly believe Jesus is our Lord and Savior, the need to share Him with others is essential. Through sharing we afford others the opportunity to enter into a relationship with Him. If what the Bible says about Christ is true, our message is the most important one ever known to man. Because our message is true, sharing it with others is the greatest gift, the greatest act of kindness and love, we can extend to others.

Beyond all other reasons for sharing Christ, the Lord Himself commanded us to do so, saying:

> All authority has been given to Me in heaven and on earth. Go therefore and make disciples of all the nations, baptizing them in the name of the Father and of the Son and of the Holy Spirit, teaching them to observe all things that I have commanded you. (Matthew 28:18-20)

All believers are commanded to "Go therefore and make disciples," but for the truly faithful this is a labor of love. In and through it we prove our love for Christ as well as our love for a world in need of spiritual healing.

The Goal of the Call

We are not commanded to put off the old self and put on the new self, learn, live and lend God's Word for no reason. Behind the call the believer is striving after a special goal: "true righteousness and holiness" (Ephesians 4:24).

At the heart of all our endeavors is a desire to be like God. Paul noted two ways in which we are to be like Him. First, we are to enmesh ourselves with His "righteousness." In essence, Paul was saying, "Be like God in all areas of your life. Let His rightness be your rightness."

The second part of the goal is to be like God as related to His "holiness." The word *holy* indicates a setting apart from evil and worldliness. The believer in Christ is called to separate himself from those things that detract from becoming more like Christ.

This does not mean we attempt to sever ourselves from those around us. Rather we are to minister to all while being mastered by none. Our lives must be characterized by a righteous and holy passion, absorbed in being like and pleasing our Master, the Lord Jesus Christ.

7 The Comforter's Care

The ministry Jesus Christ accomplished while on earth established the means by which man could obtain spiritual healing. As our spiritual Physician, He realized that man needed more than healing and spiritual tools to succeed. Therefore, Jesus promised the Comforter who would come and care for the spiritual therapy and development of His followers.

Jesus said, "The Comforter, which is the Holy Ghost [or Holy Spirit] the Father will send in My name" (John 14:26 KJV). The Comforter Jesus spoke of was commissioned by God the Father and was sent on the day of Pentecost as promised. Scripture says:

> And suddenly there came a sound from heaven, as of a rushing mighty wind, and it filled the whole house where they were sitting. Then there appeared to them divided tongues, as of fire, and one sat upon each of them. And they were all filled with the Holy Spirit. (Acts 2:2-4)

Through the empowering of the Holy Spirit, men who days earlier sheepishly sat huddled together "for fear of the Jews" (John

20:19) were transformed into brave and mighty men of God. In fact, they became men of such high caliber, they would one day stand in the presence of religious and governmental leaders, as well as angry crowds, to faithfully proclaim the gospel of Christ.

Someone lacking all the facts might be led to honor these men for their accomplishments, but this would be a mistake. The achievements were not theirs, but the Holy Spirit's. Their knowledge, courage, and drive had nothing to do with good genes or hard work, but rather an awesome God who provided the Comforter and Counselor supreme.

The Comforter—Who Is He?

Who is the Holy Spirit, the Comforter promised by God? He is the third Person of the Trinity—the Father, Son and Holy Spirit. As with the other members of the Trinity, the Holy Spirit is a personal being. He is not simply a force or power. As a person, the Bible describes Him as having intelligence (John 14:26; Romans 8:16), a will (Acts 16:7; 1 Corinthians 12:11), and affection (Isaiah 63:10; Ephesians 4:30). Like the Father and the Son, He performs various personal acts. He searches (1 Corinthians 2:10), speaks (Revelation 2:7), testifies (John 15:26), and convicts (John 16:8-11). The Comforter maintains a personal relationship with all true believers.

The Comforter—Where Is He?

The Bible makes it clear that the Holy Spirit is a living Being. This leads us to ask, "Where is He?" At the point of salvation, the Comforter joins Himself with the new believer in Christ, permanently indwelling him. The Bible says, "Do you not know that your body is the temple of the Holy Spirit who is in you, whom you have from God?" (1 Corinthians 6:19).

One of the most precious and important gifts bestowed on the believer is the indwelling of the Holy Spirit. In the Old Testament we see clear evidence of His presence in the lives of the saints, but not to the point it is seen in the New Testament.

In the New Testament, once the Spirit establishes His presence, He permanently indwells the believer. In the Old Testament the

Spirit came upon the believer, but did not permanently abide in him. This becomes evident when King David said, "Do not cast me away from Your presence, and do not take Your Holy Spirit from me" (Psalms 51:11). David was truly fearful of losing the presence and ministry of the Spirit in his life. Because Christians are sealed by the Spirit (2 Corinthians 1:22; Ephesians 1:13-14; 4:30), assurance of His ongoing presence and the salvation that accompanies it (1 John 5:11-13) are both certain. As a result, the believer in Christ has hope. We need not wrestle with the fear expressed by David, but rather rejoice in knowing He is ours and we are His forevermore.

The Wonderful Wonder of the Indwelling Spirit

There is a wonderful "wonder" that accompanies the presence of the Holy Spirit in the life of the physically impaired.

For those who have experienced the painful darts of prejudice or who have been made to feel abnormal, the good news is, the Holy Spirit does not view the physically impaired through the narrow framework of a disability. Once we become a child of God, the true abnormality—spiritual impairment—has been remedied. In God's eyes all His spiritual offspring become whole and wholesome in a way few others will ever know.

When God looks upon the spiritually healed yet physically impaired, He is not repulsed by their physical condition. The Lord is far more interested in the condition of a person's heart than his physical body.

An athlete may develop a beautifully sculpted body, be physically strong and a delight to behold, but if he has never entered into a true relationship with Jesus Christ, from God's perspective he is a spiritual "quadriplegic." The Bible says, "Cursed is the man who trusts in man and makes flesh his strength, whose heart departs from the Lord" (Jeremiah 17:5). One's physical strength and mental capacity is not the guiding factor in God's determination of worth. God "searches the minds and hearts" of men (1 Chronicles 28:9; Jeremiah 17:10; Revelation 2:23) to determine such things.

Because of this wonderful "wonder," the physically impaired are able to find a level of relevance and worth otherwise unknown to them. Even though men may reject and look down on the impaired, God wants to heal them spiritually and embrace them eternally through His free gift of salvation. And to those who partake of it, the Comforter will come to reside and minister in their hearts.

The Comforter and His Care

One of the key responsibilities of the Comforter is to care for God's spiritual children. Jesus promised His disciples He would never leave them "as orphans" (John 14:18). He promised to send the "Spirit of truth" (John 14:17) to care for them. Let's take a look at some of the ways the Holy Spirit accomplishes this.

Care through Conviction

One of the most basic aspects of the Spirit's ministry is convicting man of his sin (John 16:8-11). When engaged in this aspect of ministry, the Holy Spirit sensitizes us to see sin problems in our lives. This recognition may lead a person to experience a sense of grief and emotional pain.

The Bible says, "God is love." If God is the epitome of love, why does He allow the Spirit to bring grief and pain upon us? In short, because He truly does love us and wants to care for us.

When I broke my heel, due to the severity of its condition, my surgeon encouraged me to consider the long-term consequences of skipping surgery. After explaining the importance of immediate surgery, he pointed out that I should be prepared to experience several months of pain and discomfort.

If I was going to experience significant pain with or without surgery, why have surgery? Simply put, by recognizing the severity of the problem and dealing with it right away, the pain would eventually pass and bring greater healing. Without surgery, the problem would continue to plague me for the rest of my life.

Why did my surgeon encourage me to face the long-term realities of my problem and deal with it, even if it meant a painful recovery? Because he genuinely cared about my welfare. As my physician, he wanted what was best for me. He knew that a few months of physical suffering was better than years of it. He could have ignored the problem and allowed me to suffer, but he didn't because he truly cared and wanted what was best for me.

Why does the Holy Spirit convict us of our sin? Because like my surgeon He knows, apart from acknowledging the problem, there is no hope of dealing with it—consequently, spiritual healing remains impossible. Thus, the Spirit convicts us of our sin, not for the purpose of harming us, but as a first step in the healing of our souls.

Care through Renewal

A second element of the Holy Spirit's ministry involves the spiritual renewal (regeneration) of man. All men are born into this world spiritually dead to God. David said, "Surely I was sinful at birth, sinful from the time my mother conceived me" (Psalm 51:5 NIV). Some may wonder how David could have viewed himself "sinful at birth." To answer this question, one need only consider what a "sinner" is. Essentially, a sinner is someone whose personal motivation is rooted in pleasing self rather than God. Pleasing self above God is at the heart of all sin.

The nature described by David testifies to the certainty of man's spiritual deadness. Because of it, man in and of himself is not capable of maintaining a relationship with God. The prophet Isaiah noted the destructive influence of sin when describing Israel's wrongdoing, saying, "Your iniquities have separated you from your God; and your sins have hidden His face from you, so that He will not hear" (Isaiah 59:2). Sin separates all men from God (Romans 3:23) and renders a healthy relationship with Him impossible.

The good news is that the Holy Spirit is also capable of bringing about a complete renewal of the deadened sinner's heart. This results in an awakening from the bondage of spiritual death to the newness and freedom of spiritual life.

The Bible refers to this renewal in many ways. Jesus said to Nicodemus (a religious leader of His day), "Most assuredly, I say to you, unless one is born again, he cannot see the kingdom of God" (John 3:3). Jesus used the phrase "born again" to in part describe the sort of spiritual transformation a person must undergo in order to make eternal fellowship with God possible.

Scripture also associates renewal with becoming a new creation. The Bible says, "Therefore, if anyone is in Christ, he is a new creation; old things have passed away; behold, all things have become new" (2 Corinthians 5:17). Here Scripture points out that spiritual renewal not only encompasses a second birth, it also includes becoming an entirely new spiritual creature. The Bible extends this thought one step further, saying, "God, who is rich in mercy, because of His great love with which He loved us, even when we were dead in trespasses, made us alive together with Christ" (Ephesians 2:4-5). Here renewal is depicted as a resurrection from spiritual death to spiritual life.

Each of these passages features a dramatic change from spiritual paralysis to spiritual vitality. Is change of this magnitude possible apart from divine intervention? Certainly not. Just as it is impossible for man to will himself into physical birth, it is impossible for him to do so spiritually. The act of rebirth, re-creation, and resurrection from spiritual death are elements belonging not to man or earthly science, but solely to the ministry of the Holy Spirit. Only the Spirit is capable of breathing spiritual newness into the heart of sinful man. Apart from the Holy Spirit's caring ministry, man is spiritually without hope.

Renewal is the foundation upon which the believer's salvation rests. It occurs instantaneously and is a result of faith in the Lord Jesus. It is not something man is capable of earning, but is a product of God's grace. At the time of renewal, man's old sin nature is replaced by a new nature "patterned after the nature of God Himself."[1] Prior to spiritual renewal, man's motivation was rooted in pleasing self, but through renewal, man is found longing "after the things of God."[2] Accordingly, the desire to please and maintain a relationship with Him becomes a reality.

The effects of renewal are many. Each are inseparable from the act of renewal. As renewal occurs, things like faith, repentance, justification, and adoption take place instantaneously.

As a result of the renewal wrought by the Holy Spirit, aspects such as His indwelling, sealing, baptism (uniting) into the body of Christ, filling, etc., are made possible as well.

---

1. Lewis S. Chafer, *Major Bible Themes*, p. 99.
2. Chafer, p. 99.

Care through Cultivation

Once a person has received salvation, the Holy Spirit begins to spiritually cultivate and refine him. Practically speaking, this process, referred to as sanctification, takes many forms and is lifelong in nature. The objective during this phase of the Spirit's ministry is to establish the image of Christ in all areas of the person's life. The ideal is to live, act, and be as Christ was. There are several ways in which the Holy Spirit helps the believer become more like Jesus.

The Filling of the Holy Spirit

Earlier we spoke of the necessity of putting off the old man or self, and putting on the new (Ephesians 4:22-24), the old being the life lived prior to a relationship with Jesus Christ; the new being a life characterized by Christlikeness. By what means does a true follower of Christ obtain the ability to do so? Where does the strength come from? Is it simply a matter of trying harder or believing more than someone else? No. The ability to become more like Christ goes far beyond mere human determination.

The cultivation process is begun and accomplished through the ministry of the Holy Spirit in the life of the believer. The ability to become more like Jesus is a result of the filling of the Holy Spirit. When describing the essence of what it means to be Spirit filled, Charles C. Ryrie said, "Filling means control—100 percent control of all known matters and areas of the Christian's life."[3]

At the heart of the Spirit-filled life is the willingness on the part of a believer to allow the Holy Spirit to have control over all aspects of his life. The battle for control over a Christian's life is primarily waged in the heart and mind. The degree to which he is committed to recognizing and confessing his sin will determine the degree to which the Spirit maintains control. If a person gives in to sinful desires and repeatedly fails to confess and seek cleansing and forgiveness from God, through his actions he allows sin rather than the Holy Spirit to have control over his life. Sin stifles the ministry of the Spirit; true confession and repen-

---

3. Charles C. Ryrie, *The Holy Spirit*, p. 103.

tance (turning from sin to God) encourages the Spirit's ministry and control in the believer's life.

Ephesians 5:18 describes the war waged in the heart and mind of the Christian saying, "Do not be drunk with wine, in which is dissipation; but be filled with the Spirit." Even though the sin of drunkenness is used here, we may consider it to represent sin in general. Yet of all the sins man may commit, perhaps more than most, drunkenness provides a graphic example of sin's inner and outer control over a person. When a Christian allows himself to become drunk, alcohol controls him, not the Holy Spirit.

Certainly, all sin, regardless of degree, interferes with the Spirit's ministry of filling. The Bible brings this out when it says:

> Walk in the Spirit, and you shall not fulfill the lust of the flesh. For the flesh lusts against the Spirit, and the Spirit against the flesh; and these are contrary to one another, so that you do not do the things that you wish. (Galatians 5:16-17)

Every time a believer chooses to sin, he renders both heart and mind to the controlling power of sin rather than that of the Holy Spirit. Thankfully, God has provided confession and repentance to break sin's dominion over our lives.

Scripture commands believers to "be filled with the Spirit" (Ephesians 5:18) and to "walk [live] in the Spirit" (Galatians 5:16) so they may maintain a consistent and harmonious walk with Christ. This in turn enables Christians to progressively exhibit a greater likeness of Christ in and through their lives.

The Holy Spirit's Ministry of Teaching

Once we are eternally bound by the loving embrace of the Comforter, He begins to carefully reconstruct our frame of reference by encouraging the growth and reeducation of the new believer in the ways of God through the Scriptures.

The Holy Spirit's ministry of teaching was promised by the Lord when He said:

> However, when He, the Spirit of truth, has come, He will guide you into all truth; for He will not speak on His own authority, but whatever He hears He will speak; and He will

tell you things to come. He will glorify Me, for He will take of what is Mine and declare it to you. (John 16:13-14)

We see a clear confirmation of this when Paul said, "These things we also speak, not in words which man's wisdom teaches but which the Holy Spirit teaches, comparing spiritual things with spiritual" (1 Corinthians 2:13).

Here, one of history's most prominent Bible teachers states that his source of instruction was not a product of human wisdom, but the Holy Spirit Himself. In doing so, he refuses to lend even the smallest ounce of credit to man, for it belongs solely to God.

The apostle John also attests to the presence of the Holy Spirit's teaching ministry, saying:

> But the anointing which you have received from Him abides in you, and you do not need that anyone teach you; but as the same anointing teaches you concerning all things, and is true, and is not a lie, and just as it has taught you, you will abide in Him. (1 John 2:27)

John warned believers to abandon any thought of following or even listening to the instruction of false teachers. He referred to them as "antichrists" (1 John 2:18) for through their teaching they denied "Jesus is the Christ" (1 John 2:22). Because their teachings had upset the faith of some, in the strongest terms John encouraged the church to disregard such teaching. Why? Because "the same anointing teaches you concerning all things, and is true, and is not a lie."

Because the believer is joined to the Teacher of teachers, there is no need to consider the heretical teachings or special insights false teachers claim to possess. Why entertain a lie when the truth lives within you? Why embrace foolishness over wisdom? Why play with fire when you can study Scripture itself?

Clearly, there is no reason, for "the same anointing teaches you concerning all things." It is real, it is active, it is everything one needs to grasp God's truth and recognize those godly teachers appointed by Him to act as shepherds over His flock.

The Holy Spirit's Ministry of Leading

Closely associated with the Holy Spirit's teaching ministry is His ministry of leading. This ministry is portrayed in the Spirit's oversight in the life of the believer. Jesus said, "When He, the Spirit of truth, has come, He will guide you into all truth" (John 16:13). The truth spoken of here is not characterized by secrets or mysteries. Rather, it is witnessed in the Scriptures. Therefore, the believer need not seek out the leading of the deceased as King Saul did (1 Samuel 28), for Paul said, "For as many as are led by the Spirit of God, these are sons of God" (Romans 8:14). As much as the leading of the Spirit is a proof of a believer's sonship, sonship brings with it the leading of the Holy Spirit.

This ministry of guidance begins at the time of a believer's spiritual birth and continues throughout the course of his life. Because the Spirit indwells the believer, access to His leading is available twenty-four hours a day.

As willing and able as the Holy Spirit is, His involvement is contingent on the believer's personal consistency and faithfulness. The Holy Spirit will never direct, encourage, or condone sin, and yet He does not force people to refrain from it.

His leading is most effective when Christians are in harmony with God and His Word. Hence, the choice is clear and simple. Faithfulness to God enables the Spirit to faithfully lead us. Sinfulness stifles His effectiveness and ability to guide us. Consequently, we must strive with all our hearts to maintain personal purity. If we fall short, we should go to the Lord immediately and earnestly seek out cleansing, forgiveness, and restoration. In doing so, we preserve our standing and allow the Holy Spirit to faithfully lead us in the ways of righteousness.

The Holy Spirit's Ministry of Intercession

Not only does the Holy Spirit engage in teaching and leading believers, He also intercedes on our behalf. The Bible speaks of the Spirit's ministry of intercession, saying:

> Likewise the Spirit also helps in our weaknesses. For we do not know what we should pray for as we ought, but the Spirit Himself makes intercession for us with groanings which can-

not be uttered. Now He who searches the hearts knows what the mind of the Spirit is, because He makes intercession for the saints according to the will of God. (Romans 8:26-27)

It is interesting to note that the Bible classifies all believers as those maintaining a measure of weakness. In other words, whether a person is a spiritual giant or just a babe, spiritually we are found wanting. All believers—regardless of title, role, or even physical makeup—need the Holy Spirit to help our prayers become acceptable. Why? Because all of us are spiritually lacking in our ability to pray.

The frail process of human thought and words is of such a nature that the Spirit's ministry of intercession is essential. When we pray, the Holy Spirit reaches deep into the wells of our souls and draws forth that which is far beyond mere words and thoughts. He takes what is lacking and "with groanings which cannot be uttered" offers up that which is beautifully acceptable and "according to the will of God."

Free at Last!

One of the most exhilarating speeches of the twentieth century was given by Dr. Martin Luther King Jr. when he uttered those famous words "I have a dream." Within the speech Dr. King proclaimed the words of an old "Negro spiritual" saying: "Free at last! Free at last! Thank God Almighty! Free at last!"

One of the greatest blessings Christianity has to offer is that of freedom and equality. Prior to salvation, the physically impaired gained "equality" only through the narrow scope of the legislative process. Upon acceptance of Jesus Christ as Savior, absolute freedom and equality become theirs for all eternity.

The physically impaired are made free and equal through Christ's death and resurrection. Freedom and equality are also witnessed through the ongoing ministry of teaching, leading, and intercession imparted by the Holy Spirit. These gifts are freely given to impaired and unimpaired alike, for as the apostle Peter said, "In truth I perceive that God shows no partiality. But in every nation whoever fears Him and works righteousness is accepted by Him" (Acts 10:34-35). By extension we might add that God accepts men from every sort of physical condition who fear Him and do what is right, for He does not show partiality. He grants freedom and equality to all who enter into His salvation.

The blessing of blessings is that in Christ the barriers that have long separated the physically impaired from the rest of mankind have been done away with. At the cross of our Lord, all prejudice, humiliation, and impairments have been abolished. Therefore, all those who have entered into an eternal relationship with Christ may joyously proclaim, "Free at last! Free at last! Thank God Almighty! Free at last!"

8 The Fellowship Factor

Life and hope exist beyond the barriers encountered by the physically impaired. Through Christ we have victory, purpose, and the ever-present Comforter. As full and rich as these blessings are, there is another gift we have yet to discuss—I refer to it as the fellowship factor.

At the heart of the fellowship factor is a single common thread that binds all true believers together; that thread is the risen Savior, Jesus Christ. The victory, purpose, comfort, and direction Christianity offers is wrapped in the holy garment of worship and exaltation of Christ and His Word.

As Lord and Master of the Church, Christ not only unites believers in the marriage of true fellowship, He presides over it as well. Thus, for fellowship to maintain a sense of relevance and validity, we must make certain Christ is the center of our fellowship in thought, word, and deed.

You might find yourself wondering, *What's the big deal? What makes fellowship so important?* Beside the fact that Christ commanded believers to partake in it, the fellowship factor creates a sense of community. This helps all believers, impaired and unimpaired, to understand that they are not alone, but are part of a spiritual family.

The benefits of belonging to this holy household are many. Ecclesiastes 4:9-10 says:

> Two are better than one, because they have a good reward for their labor. For if they fall, one will lift up his companion. But woe to him who is alone when he falls, for he has no one to help him up.

Here the Bible helps us reflect on the benefits derived from friendship: greater effectiveness in accomplishing tasks, caring for and helping one another, and the like.

One of the greatest blessings surrounding the fellowship factor is that the Lord has directed all believers to maintain a degree of interdependence and care for one another. This takes on added significance for believers who are physically impaired.

The Least of These

Prior to Christ's crucifixion He gave us an amazing glimpse into the future. In the gospel of Matthew the Lord said:

> When the Son of Man comes in His glory, and all the holy angels with Him, then He will sit on the throne of His glory. All the nations will be gathered before Him, and He will separate them one from another, as a shepherd divides his sheep from the goats. And He will set the sheep on His right hand, but the goats on the left. Then the King will say to those on His right hand, "Come, you blessed of My Father, inherit the kingdom prepared for you from the foundation of the world: for I was hungry and you gave Me food; I was thirsty and you gave Me drink; I was a stranger and you took Me in; I was naked and you clothed Me; I was sick and you visited Me; I was in prison and you came to Me." Then the righteous will answer Him, saying, "Lord, when did we see You hungry and feed You, or thirsty and give You drink? When did we see You a stranger and take You in, or naked and clothe You? Or when did we see You sick, or in prison, and come to You?" And the

King will answer and say to them, "Assuredly, I say to you, inasmuch as you did it to one of the least of these My brethren, you did it to Me." (Matthew 25:31-40)

In this passage the Lord spoke of a time when He will return to separate His true followers from those who are not. In Matthew chapter 25 verse 40 the Lord identified a special characteristic true followers display while here on earth. He says, "Assuredly, I say to you, inasmuch as you did it to one of the least of these My brethren, you did it to Me." Jesus linked sincere acts of caring and interdependence toward fellow believers as gestures specifically directed at Him. From His perspective, these acts of love and support stand as proofs of the validity of a disciple's association with Him.

Sadly, within this passage we see believers who were hungry, thirsty, sick, in need of clothes, and even in prison because of their faith. These depictions help us understand that even good and godly people at times encounter hardships. It also reminds us that we must be careful not to rush to judgment when considering the source of a fellow believer's troubles. It is easy to fool ourselves into believing we know why a tragedy has befallen someone, but apart from knowing the mind of God, such things are difficult, if not impossible, to grasp.

This passage offers one additional bit of information we must consider. It appears in Jesus' statement, "I was sick and you visited Me." This phrase identifies a category I will refer to as the "sick." The "sick" may include all believers suffering from some sort of physical ailment or impairment.

When considering Christ's discourse, a measure of hope springs forth for all those battling various afflictions. The hope is seen in the fact that God Himself identifies with people such as this. Through His assertion, Jesus united Himself with the sick and the physically impaired. It is as if He were saying, "The sick and the physically impaired who are my disciples, are one with Me. As a result, everyone who ministers to them is likewise ministering to Me."

Jesus is often pictured as a shepherd. As a faithful and true Shepherd, Jesus loves His sheep with the deepest of love. He made this clear when He said:

> What man of you, having a hundred sheep, if he loses one of them, does not leave the ninety-nine in the wilderness, and go after the one which is lost until he finds it? And when he has found it, he lays it on his shoulders, rejoicing. (Luke 15:4-6)

What a beautiful picture of a caring and loving Savior wrapping His arms around the lost and hurting children of this world, picking them up one by one and carrying their frail frames safely home.

As the good Shepherd, Jesus delights in those who love and care for His "sheep." He considers it to be a trait that should be found in all true believers. To Jesus, caring for others is not an exceptional quality, but a common practice. Why? Because if the Spirit of God truly resides in the heart of a person, he will be compelled to love and care for others, even as the good Shepherd did.

This is wonderful news for the physically impaired. For with the fellowship factor comes a loving and caring spiritual family—a family that spans throughout the world, as well as throughout the ages and ages to come. This family is called to rejoice together (Philippians 4:4), suffer together (1 Corinthians 12:26), and care for its own (Romans 12:13; 2 Corinthians 9:13; Galatians 6:6). Why? Because as the Bible points out, "With such sacrifices God is well pleased" (Hebrews 13:16). Pleasing God through concrete expressions of love is what the fellowship factor is all about. One day Jesus will gloriously proclaim with all authority, "Assuredly, I say to you, inasmuch as you did it to one of the least of these My brethren, you did it to Me."

Barriers and Bridges

One way today's church can seek to accomplish this calling to love is by building bridges to the physically impaired and helping destroy barriers that stand in their way.

Prior to obtaining my impairment, I was blind to the struggles the physically impaired encounter. On a daily basis, the impaired struggle with things that are second nature to the unimpaired. Unfortunately, it took physical impairment for me to become more aware of such things.

In far too many cases, Christians are slow to respond to the needs and concerns of the physically impaired. Rather than aggressively seeking to build bridges and destroy barriers within the local assembly, too often we have been satisfied with business as usual. Nevertheless, the church and its people are commanded by Christ to maintain a higher standard.

What are some ways society and the local church inadvertently harm the physically impaired?

Stigmatization

By definition a stigmatism is a physical, personal, or social "mark" an individual may bear in one way or another. In a very real sense, the physically impaired daily bear the personal and social "marks" of their impairment.

We get a better sense of the social stigma surrounding such things when we consider the experiences of a woman named Patricia Moore. At the age of twenty-six, she decided to disguise herself as an eighty-five-year-old woman in order to determine how society treats the elderly. To help create a sense of reality Ms. Moore smeared baby oil under her contact lenses to blur her vision, wore earplugs to deaden her hearing, taped her fingers and covered them with cotton gloves to simulate arthritis, and wrapped her legs in such a way as to severely stifle her mobility.

Ms. Moore's disguise was so convincing, those around her actually thought she was an elderly woman struggling with various age-related impairments. To her dismay she repeatedly experienced the stigmatizing effects of both age and impairment. As a young and healthy woman, people tended to treat her with respect, but as an impaired eight-five-year-old, people were impatient, condescending, disrespectful, and at times cruel.[1]

The treatment Ms. Moore received was nothing more than a by-product of the vast stigmatic shadow cast upon the elderly and the physically impaired daily. In part this is due to the imbalance and insensitivity that pervades society as a whole.

---

1. Deborah Sharp, "Young author lives life of an old lady - The Patricia Moore Story," *Gannett News Service*, (1985) pp. B5, B7.

As described in *The Handicap Plea,* the physically impaired identify well with the social stigma Ms. Moore experienced. Thus, we must assume there is a real problem here. People are not simply feeling sorry for themselves, nor crying over "spilled milk." Rather, in a very real way, the physically impaired suffer from the effects of stigmatic barriers rendered by society.

Unlike the world in general, the church of Jesus Christ has been commissioned to build bridges to our physically impaired brothers and sisters. Therefore, within our local assemblies we must lovingly strive to cleanse ourselves of all thoughts and opinions that stigmatize any of Christ's children. For some, this may mean thinking twice before telling a joke where the impaired are made fun of. For others, it may mean carefully thinking through and reshaping their views of the physically impaired. Regardless of what it takes, the church is called to build bridges and tear down stigmatic barriers.

Generalizations

A second barrier confronting the physically impaired is that of generalizations. When learning about people and their circumstances, some tend to form generalizations surrounding the whats and wherefores of the people. Often such generalizations are formed apart from concrete and substantive facts. The fabric of the assumptions may be nothing more than mental snapshots acquired over a period of time.

There is nothing wrong with forming mild generalizations, as no one is capable of interacting with every detail encountered. But if we are going to build bridges to those with special needs, we must avoid generalizations that distort our sense of reality.

The problem with some generalizations is, they tend to corrosively eat away at a person's individuality. How? By placing people into neat little boxes. Within these boxes everyone acts the same, feels the same, looks the same, and for the most part is the same. This may be fine for those studying lifeless objects, but not for those called to minister to humans created in God's image.

The church is called to build bridges and eliminate barriers. Imbalanced generalizations do little more than encourage needless barriers.

How do we right this wrong? We strive to see people as God sees them—one person at a time. As ministers of Christ we must avoid the practice of forming generalizations about various people groups. When tempted to believe all young, old, black, white, heavy, thin, impaired or unimpaired people are . . . (fill in the blank), make the effort to see people as unique individuals wonderfully created by God Himself.

Limitations

Another potential barrier confronting the physically impaired is that of limitations. The limitations I speak of are not those resulting from impairments, but those thrust upon the physically impaired by well-intentioned people.

At times people can express too much concern over the impairments of others—so much so, they make it impossible for the physically impaired to make meaningful contributions to the work of the ministry. This is like a mother who loves her children so much, she never allows them to play for fear of hurting themselves. This sort of treatment results in imbalanced children. In similar fashion, some churches have unknowingly limited the role of the physically impaired simply by failing to encourage their involvement in ministry-related activities.

Whether we limit the role of the impaired because we do not want to overtax them, or because we lack the patience and flexibility to allow such things, the church and the impaired are ultimately done a disservice. By discouraging their participation, we encourage their stagnation rather than their growth. The physically impaired need to be included. If they are true believers in Christ, they have as much a part in the Lord's ministry as anyone else.

Personal Treatment

A common barrier that must not be overlooked is that of personal treatment. How do we treat the physically impaired within our local church? Do we make them feel a part of the common fellowship? Are they made to feel like coworkers and equal partners in the work of the ministry? Are their contributions acknowledged as valuable to the direction of the church?

Imagine yourself walking into your home one afternoon and your spouse and children began treating you not as family, but as a welcomed guest. How would you feel? A bit strange or out of place? Why? Because your family is treating you in an unusual manner. Let's face it, no matter how welcome and polite others may be, if someone is friendly, yet distant, interested, but not really concerned, present, but certainly not involved, mere words and politeness will never convince you that you are truly part of the family.

Physical impairment does not equate to emotional or intellectual impairment. The physically impaired may have certain bodily limitations, but this does not mean they cannot sense when they are being treated as something less than family. The daily difficulties of a physical impairment can weigh heavily upon a person. Are we lightening the emotional load or adding to it? Are we treating such people with open-armed love and true kinship? Are we providing them with a bridge or just another invisible barrier?

The Church Building

The last barrier we will consider is that of the church building. This can be a touchy area because many church buildings are old and even minor structural changes can prove costly. As much as some churches may long to accommodate the needs of the physically impaired, many are severely strapped due to financial constraints. However, as resources become available, we ought to consider what we can do to make our church buildings more suited to the needs of the physically impaired.

Accessibility

When considering alterations, renovations, or new construction of a church facility, it is essential to consider how the change will affect the physically impaired. In doing so, we may spare ourselves needless headaches and costly expenses later.

As is sometimes the case, when formulating building plans, some may believe such considerations to be a waste of time. They may argue that the number of physically impaired who attend the church is so small, special consideration is not worth the effort.

There are at least three reasons churches and building committees should avoid embracing this sort of thinking. The most obvious reason is that we do not know what the future makeup of the congregation will be. At any point, one or more people attending a church may enter the ranks of the physically impaired through illness, accident, or old age. And lest we forget, all of us have the potential to fall prey to such things ourselves. Thus, considering the needs of the physically impaired is nothing more than responsibly planning for the future needs of the church body.

A second reason it is wise to consider the needs of the physically impaired is outreach. Imagine each car passing your church represents a family in search of a new place to worship. As they drive by, they survey the building to determine its accessibility for one member is severely impaired. Would your building encourage them to stop and visit or continue searching for a church that can meet this basic requirement?

By considering the needs of the physically impaired, we create many more opportunities to welcome and minister to families and individuals within our community. On the other hand, when we fail to consider such things, it is like posting a sign on the church lawn saying, "The physically impaired are not welcome here."

One last consideration we must keep in mind is that of empathy. Whenever we find ourselves making long-term decisions that affect the lives of the physically impaired, it is wise to ask ourselves how we might feel about this decision if we were physically impaired. Of course we can only carry this thinking so far, but approaching decisions through the eyes of another may help us make more balanced decisions. Jesus taught us to "love your neighbor as yourself" (Matthew 22:39) and "whatever you want men to do to you, do also to them" (Matthew 7:12). The Lord's strong admonition to consider the welfare of others should be applied to all areas of life. In the most practical sense, this exhortation would even include such things as building accessibility.

Building Maintenance and Grounds Keeping

Along with accessibility, it is important we keep our building and grounds well maintained. Some basic concerns we should keep in mind include:

Temperature of the Building

Low temperatures can have a severe effect on certain types of physical impairments. Therefore, it is important for those who care for the maintenance of the building to make certain that prior to a meeting, the room temperature is suitable for everyone attending.

Impediments in and outside the Building

For those with young children, the presence of clutter may be a common sight. But for those who have a physical impairment that either partially or totally limits their mobility, clutter becomes an obstacle, or worse yet a source of potential danger.

Inside a church, books, toys, clothing, etc. may easily find their way to the floor or on the pews. Outside the building, garbage, rocks, branches and small tree limbs, snow, ice, etc. may collect on walkways, parking lots, and lawns. For those using aids such as canes, crutches, prosthetic limbs, or wheel chairs, even very small objects can impede their ability to move from place to place. Attempting to navigate around such things can cause needless anxiety and fatigue.

Structural Stability

Another important aspect we must consider is that of structural stability. I once visited a church that had constructed a wood ramp to assist the physically impaired. It was wonderful that the church cared enough to do this for those in need. Unfortunately, the structure was not stable. The wood used for the walkway was not treated and had begun to rot. One section had rotted to the point that it had developed a three-inch hole. From my perspective, the ramp was unsafe for both the impaired and unimpaired. The church had meant well, but their ramp was a safety hazard for everyone.

Some may be tempted to blame this on the pastor or the grounds committee, but it's the responsibility of the entire church to make certain all ramps, walkways, chairs, pews, and the like are safe. Such things reflect on the entire church, not simply on a pastor or a committee. Why? Because in the event someone is badly hurt, depending on the circumstances and prevailing law, the church and/or its membership may be held legally accountable.[2] Thus, for the sake of all participants, each of us must be committed to maintaining a safe and well-kept environment.

The Americans with Disabilities Act (ADA)

One of the most significant pieces of legislation to come out of Washington, DC is the *Americans with Disabilities Act*. It covers things such as Employment Provisions and Equal Employment Opportunity (Title I), State and Local Government Programs and Services (Title II), and information regarding Public Accommodations and Commercial Facilities (Title III).

The Act is important because it establishes specific guidelines for the proper treatment of those who struggle with various types of restrictive disabilities. The ADA's goal is to create a measure of equality within society and the workplace for those with disabilities. The ADA can be an insightful educational tool for all those seeking to further the cause of the physically impaired.

Within the ADA, Sec. 307, "Exemptions For Private Clubs and Religious Organizations (42 USC 12187)," states the provisions of the title do not apply to "religious organizations or entities controlled by religious organizations, including places of worship."

In short, churches are not held accountable by law to enact the various physical requirements found in Title III of the ADA. Although this is good news for churches struggling to keep the doors open, it should not be considered a reason to ignore the practical relevance of the ADA. Whether accountable or not, churches should strive to the best of their ability to upgrade their facilities to practically complement the limitations of the physically impaired.

In addition to the suggestions mentioned earlier, the Technical Manual for Title III of the ADA gives twenty-one examples of modifications that may prove helpful to church buildings:

---

2. Laws governing bodily injury resulting from church negligence are distinct from those established under the ADA. Bodily injury cases are considered tort liability which varies by state.

- Installing ramps
- Making curb cuts in sidewalks and entrances
- Repositioning shelves
- Rearranging tables, chairs, vending machines, display racks, and other furniture
- Repositioning telephones
- Adding raised markings on elevator control buttons
- Installing flashing alarm lights
- Widening doors
- Installing offset hinges to widen doorways
- Eliminating a turnstile or providing an alternative accessible path
- Installing accessible door hardware
- Rearranging toilet stalls
- Rearranging toilet partitions to increase maneuvering space
- Insulating lavatory pipes under sinks to prevent burns
- Installing raised toilet seats
- Installing a full-length bathroom mirror
- Repositioning the paper towel dispenser in the bathroom
- Creating designated accessible parking spaces
- Installing an accessible paper cup dispenser at an existing inaccessible water fountain
- Removing high-pile, low-density carpeting
- Installing vehicle hand controls

The average church lacks the necessary resources to implement the entirety of this list. But some of the recommendations are basic and inexpensive. Those churches looking to produce immediate results may consider prioritizing the list and chip away at it over time. As the church does so, undoubtedly the church will stand as a constant reminder of its concern and commitment as ministers to the physically impaired.

Two Perspectives on Reality

When obstacles are regularly present, the stress produced by them work to drain the physically impaired of their vitality. This occurs because the presence of such barriers work to create an environment that demands additional mental, emotional, and physical exertion. For some, this may produce a heightened awareness of the barriers regularly impeding their progress. Prolonged exposure to such things may lead some to wonder if anyone really cares about their welfare. In turn this may generate a sense of frustration, followed by hurt and even bitter feelings on the part of the impaired.

While the physically impaired may view these things as acts of insensitivity, the non-impaired may not even realize a problem exists. More often than not the real problem is one of perception, not lack of concern. It is difficult for the non-impaired to view life through the eyes of the impaired.

To some degree we may equate this to the cultural and racial struggles black and white Americans have encountered in recent generations. Many on both sides have experienced hurt, critical, and even bitter feelings toward the other. One of the major contributors to the problem is perception. Many on both sides either will not or cannot relate with the concerns of the other. Why? Because it is extremely difficult to appreciate a vantage point outside our realm of behavior and experience.

I began to realize this during a yearlong stay in Liberia, West Africa. My first real taste came when my wife and I went food shopping in the capital city of Monrovia. After we parked the car, we got out and walked into a massive crowd of black people. I immediately understood what it was like to be a minority in an unfamiliar culture. Initially I felt uncomfortable, because I was different from everyone else. But as time passed, the experience helped me become more sensitive toward minorities.

As was the case in Liberia, when I broke my heel, in a real sense, I was forced into a new culture. Without realizing it, I entered the world of the physically impaired. I could no longer use my right foot. I was forced to walk with crutches. Because pain and fear of reinjury were constantly present, every step and every movement I made was slowly and carefully calculated. To some my actions might have appeared extreme, but to me it was a form of self-preservation.

Just as I became more sensitive to minorities after becoming a minority, I became more sensitive to the physically impaired once I became impaired. All those unnoticeable barriers suddenly became obvious, and little obstacles became big ones. Things that never bothered me in the past were suddenly a source of stress and fatigue. My awareness was heightened toward those things that might hinder or even harm me.

Having had an opportunity to see life from both sides has helped me to view reality from both perspectives. Consequently, I have come to believe that when Christians display a degree of insensitivity toward others, often it is a result of their inability to perceive and comprehend that which is beyond their personal realm of experience.

Apart from first-hand experience, man in general has a difficult time grasping the struggles others face. It is not easy for us to understand what it is like to be severely impaired if we've had a consistently healthy life. Scripture brings this out when it says of Jesus, "For we do not have a High Priest who cannot sympathize with our weaknesses, but was in all points tempted as we are, yet without sin" (Hebrews 4:15). The Lord can claim a greater sense of sympathy for us because He walked in our shoes. He lived as we live and suffered as we suffer. He can say with all honesty, "I do understand, and I really do care because I have been where you are."

Practically speaking, those blessed with physical health must strive that much more to obtain a greater awareness of the concerns of the physically impaired. The essential component here is a genuine and heartfelt effort. This may mean letting down your guard and even seeking out constructive criticism. In doing so, we can learn a great deal about ourselves and those we seek to minister to.

While serving as a missionary in Liberia, I came to realize the only way I was going to adequately minister to people of an unfamiliar culture was to learn about their culture and rid myself of behavior that was offensive to them. To do so, I would have to enlist the help of a Liberian willing to point out American traits that were offensive.

One day I went to a village to meet with my friend Sagba. Upon greeting me he invited me into his home. Because of the beautiful day, I suggested we stay outside rather than sit in his one-room dwelling. Being a humble man, he did as I requested.

As time passed, I mentioned to Sagba that I wanted to become a more effective minister to his people and needed his help to do so. I pointed out that as an American, I did not understand the ways of the Liberians and was afraid I would unintentionally offend someone. I asked Sagba to inform me when he noticed offensive behavior on my part.

To my surprise, no sooner than the words passed out of my mouth, Sagba said, "There is something I would like to share with you."

I wondered what it could be. I had been very friendly and accessible to him. I had treated him fairly and as an equal. What had I done that was so bad that it would cause him to immediately point out a flaw?

Sagba said, "Do you remember when you arrived and I invited you into my room?"

"Yes," I replied.

Sagba reminded me that instead of going in, I requested we stay outside.

I told him all I wanted was to enjoy the beauty of the day.

He explained the significance of inviting me into his room. He told me that in his village the only people invited into a person's home were those considered to be true friends. Strangers are not allowed inside. Thus, my failure to go in was equivalent to telling the village that I was a stranger, not a friend.

This simple thought opened my eyes to the fact that at times there are two equally correct ways to view reality.

Clearly, if I were unwilling to open myself up to Sagba's loving criticism, in the eyes of the village, I would have come a stranger and left one as well. But because I was willing to accept his criticism, I left Sagba's house that day more equipped to minister to his people.

This principle can be applied in other situations. If a fellowship of believers desires to minister to the needs of the physically impaired, they may need to ask someone to honestly critique them. Why? Because a non-impaired person ministering to the impaired is much like a missionary ministering in a foreign culture. As a non-impaired minister of Christ, at times you are going to have cultural and intellectual blind spots. Your blind spots will be evident to the impaired, even though you cannot see them. In order to effectively minister to the physically impaired, we must be willing to learn from them.

Avenues of Encouragement

One of the most exciting and powerful tools the church has at its disposal is encouragement. As a tool, it is one of the most vital elements of the fellowship factor. As we skim through the Bible we see many examples of exhortation. It is no wonder believers are repeatedly instructed to engage in this essential ministry.

To the believer, the ministry of encouragement is not optional, for Scripture directs us to be "exhorting one another" (Hebrews 10:25). The Bible even dictates the regularity of it, saying we ought to "exhort one another daily" (Hebrews 3:13).

As important as this ministry is to the spiritual and emotional welfare of all believers, it is especially important to those who are physically impaired. The physically impaired are regularly confronted with spiritual and physical trials. This in and of itself ought to motivate us to seek out ways to strengthen and encourage believers who are physically impaired.

At first glance we may find it difficult to come up with ways to help such people, but there are many options. Let's take a look at some of the avenues we may consider.

Encouragement through Sharing the Gospel

The greatest way a Christian can encourage the physically impaired is by introducing them to the gospel of Jesus Christ. Prior to His ascension, the Lord said:

> All authority has been given to Me in heaven and on earth. Go therefore and make disciples of all the nations, baptizing them in the name of the Father and of the Son and of the Holy Spirit, teaching them to observe all things that I have commanded you; and lo, I am with you always, even to the end of the age. (Matthew 28:18-20)

When Jesus commanded us to "go therefore and make disciples of all the nations," the disciples He spoke of were not meant to come only from "all the nations," but from all backgrounds as well. One such background is the physically impaired.

To understand the importance of the physically impaired to Jesus, one need only skim through the Gospels. Time and time again we see Jesus making an effort to minister to the needs of the physically impaired. The gospel of Matthew says:

> Then His fame went throughout all Syria; and they brought to Him all sick people who were afflicted with various diseases and torments, and those who were demon-possessed, epileptics, and paralytics; and He healed them. (Matthew 4:24)

The fact that Jesus spent so much time ministering to the physically impaired helps us understand how important they are. Through personal example and direct command, the Lord makes certain we faithfully extend His gospel to the physically impaired. Without the sick, the afflicted, and the tormented being added to His church, the Lord's kingdom remains incomplete.

By accepting the gospel, the physically impaired not only obtain eternal life, but they find encouragement in the glorious change that comes with it. The benefits of order, worth, usefulness, and spiritual vitality bring hope to the most difficult circumstances. There is no greater source of encouragement we can offer than the gift of eternal life!

Encouragement through Establishing and Equipping

As wonderful a blessing as salvation is, the Lord has provided for our spiritual growth as well. The apostle Paul made this clear when he said:

> And He Himself gave some to be apostles, some prophets, some evangelists, and some pastors and teachers, for the equipping of the saints for the work of ministry, for the edifying of the body of Christ, till we all come to the unity of the faith and of the knowledge of the Son of God, to a perfect man, to the measure of the stature of the fullness of Christ. (Ephesians 4:11-13)

The Bible teaches us that the Lord provides gifted leaders within the local church for "the equipping of the saints for the work of ministry." Regardless of one's physical state, if a person is spiritually ready, willing, and able, Scripture says the Lord has provided men such as "pastors and teachers" to help establish and equip new believers for the "the work of ministry." Spiritual preparation demands at least two essential elements. First, the spiritual leadership of a local church should strive to train believers in such a way as to bring about spiritual growth and maturity. Second, as an individual develops, the training should encourage regular participation in the general work of ministry. Within the local church there are many opportunities for the physically impaired to take part in ministry. It is the responsibility of the church to encourage the impaired to participate in ministry alongside the unimpaired as often as possible.

Some of the ministries the physically impaired may partake in are: preaching, teaching, counseling, evangelism, visitation, singing, and playing instruments. Other opportunities might include leading special services centered around educating others about the role of the physically impaired in the local church, and providing special counseling and discipleship for others who are physically impaired. The only limitations that should be placed on the impaired are those areas where they are not gifted (as is the case with all believers) or areas in which their impairment makes it impossible for them to take part.

Encouragement through Spiritual Leadership

As physically impaired believers progress in spiritual maturity, spiritual leadership should be an option for them if they are qualified. Along with other potential leaders, they should be judged by the standards set forth in 1 Timothy 3:1-13 and Titus 1:5-9.

When considering men for spiritual leadership positions, churches must remember that a physical impairment does not disqualify a man from serving in the church. It is essential that we judge a person's ability to lead not by human standards, but by biblical ones. The only reasons for limiting someone's involvement should be a lack of qualifications or some sort of physical limitation that makes service impossible.

Why Include the Physically Impaired in Ministry?

Why should the physically impaired be encouraged to partake in the ministry of the local church? The most basic reason is because

Scripture does not command us to do otherwise. Apart from a clear biblical directive opposing their participation, the local church cannot justify restricting the physically impaired from taking part in some sort of ministry.

Second, one's ability to contribute to the furtherance of the church is not based on physical limitations, but on one's spiritual limitations. Because physical impairments do not tend to hinder the rate of a person's spiritual development, the ability to contribute should be determined solely on someone's rate of spiritual growth, maturity, and gifts.

Third, by excluding the physically impaired from ministry, we may rob the church of its brightest, most spiritually sound ministers. It is sad to think that the best person for a ministry might be passed over simply because he is physically impaired. This not only robs the church, it robs the individual as well. If we are genuinely striving to do what is best for the church, we must seek to maximize the gifts and talents of all believers within the church.

A fourth reason the physically impaired should be included in ministry is, in certain cases, they may be more effective than their unimpaired counterparts. In ministries such as discipleship and general counsel of the physically impaired, those with impairments may have a distinct advantage. Clearly, they benefit from the fact they are better able to relate with the struggles and concerns of impaired disciples or counselees. They can empathize in ways others cannot. This comes from the reality that they have faced and overcome trials unimpaired Christians have not. Therefore, given proper training, they may increase the overall effectiveness of church-related ministries beyond that of the non-impaired.

In addition, the physically impaired can act as role models, challenging others to progress in their spiritual growth and development. When someone with a severe impairment matures in faith, it stands as a challenge to the non-impaired. Their example boldly proclaims that if someone coping with a physical impairment can advance in Christ, everyone else is without excuse.

The church of Jesus Christ has good cause to encourage the involvement of the physically impaired within the local assembly. Beyond all else, the Lord wants the physically impaired to know they are needed and wanted in His church and ministry.

Today there are many places where the physically impaired are not wanted. As the Lord's representative, what is your response? I pray it will be one of building bridges to the physically impaired and destroying any barriers that may exist.

Other Ministries of Encouragement

If a church puts its mind to it, there are many ways it can encourage physically impaired believers. Let's take a look at some basic ways the local church can minister to them.

Visitation Ministry

One of the most common ministries in most churches is the visitation ministry. In many cases this is the responsibility of the pastor. Unfortunately, because it tends to be part of the pastor's ministry, the average Christians have come to believe they have no part in it.

As important as it is for the pastor to visit those needing care and attention, we must never forget all believers can play a vital role in this ministry. It is equally important to note that as able as pastors may be, there are others, given the opportunity, who may do just as well. As a result, the church should provide basic training and opportunities for everyone qualified to take part in this ministry.

Of course those involved in visitation must have a heart of love and compassion. It is essential that they are truly interested in ministering to the needs of others. If a person lacks spiritual maturity and balance, he may do more harm than good.

When planning the type of visitation ministry the church will provide, several things may be included to enhance the ministry. Churches looking to include more people might consider having a Sunday evening ministry night. Rather than having a regular service, the congregation could be broken down into groups with one leader (pastor, elder, etc.) and three or four others. Each group is assigned a home to visit. The group may share Scripture, pray, sing, and converse with the person they are visiting. Something like this can be a safe and enjoyable first step into ministry.

If there is a pastor or elder present, those who are visiting shut-ins may consider offering communion. Churches may also provide such services as meals-on-wheels or a book and tape library that delivers Braille literature. For those who want to make the most of visiting the shut-ins, the alternatives are many.

Regular Prayer for the Physically Impaired

Over the years I have found most people are very appreciative when the church regularly upholds them in prayer. If a church has a weekly prayer guide, it should include the names of all those maintaining severe impairments. This will remind the fellowship to keep these people in prayer, and may cause the impaired to realize others care and are supporting them.

Bible Studies Geared toward the Physically Impaired

One special way in which a church can minister to the physically impaired is by offering Bible studies geared toward them. The studies should strive to help the impaired better understand such things as their uniqueness in Christ, their role as ministers of Christ, ministries they can engage in, what it means to be a part of Christ's body, how to work through trials and difficulties, etc.

If the number of physically impaired within a congregation is minimal, the church might consider consolidating its efforts by working together with other area churches to offer such programs. The organizing church might consider dividing the sessions among the participating churches. This would minimize the workload and create a sense of variety for the participants.

Weekly Information Packets

One thing that may serve as an inspiration to the impaired who are shut-ins, is a weekly or biweekly information packet. The packet may include such things as church bulletins, inserts, minutes from church business meetings, weekly prayer guides used at the prayer meetings (this may be used to encourage shut-ins to maintain a prayer ministry for others in the church as well), and special pictures drawn for them by children during Sunday School classes.

Special Arrangements for Church-Related Activities

Special arrangements for church-related activities will vary based on the type of impairments present within the fellowship. For instance, if a congregation has one or more people who are hearing impaired, they may consider installing an earphone system in specified locations within the church. If this is not possible, a good sound system may suffice. For the deaf, some churches have been able to provide those who are skilled in "sign language" to share the message as it is preached. If no one is available, the church may consider training someone from within the church for this special ministry.

To assist shut-ins, the sick, and those who cannot attend church because of physical impairments, some churches provide members with the ability to hear services via the telephone. More recently, those with Internet connections are able to listen to recorded messages online.

For those who have difficulty walking, the church may consider roping off several pews in the rear of the sanctuary so the impaired won't have to fight the crowds to find a seat. Because of the awkwardness of wheelchairs, some churches leave extra room in the rear of the sanctuary, rather than filling it with as many pews as possible. Many newer and some older churches now provide specially designed ramps and walkways for those who have difficulty using stairs. Such things provide easy accessibility for entering and exiting the sanctuary.

Also, many churches are now designing, equipping, and locating their rest rooms with the physically impaired in mind. For those with mobility problems, the newer restrooms provide a level of accessibility the old ones do not have.

If there are some who have difficulty with vision, the church may rope off a pew or two in the front of the sanctuary. This will enable the visually impaired to better see what is going on up front. The church might consider providing large print Bibles, hymnals, and bulletins in those pews.

Small churches may find it financially impossible to provide some of these things. They might consider taking up a special monthly offering for the purpose of collecting the necessary funds to implement some of these options.

When considering all the time, money, and effort that may be spent on a small handful of people, some might wonder, "Is this really worth the effort?" The answer is yes! These people are our spiritual brothers and sisters. And lest we forget, one day we too may join the ranks of the physically impaired.

As we wrestle with these unique concerns, let us consider the words of the apostle Paul:

> Now may the God of patience and comfort grant you to be like-minded toward one another, according to Christ Jesus, that you may with one mind and one mouth glorify the God and Father of our Lord Jesus Christ. (Romans 15:5-6)

This passage applies to the entire church, not only those who are physically unimpaired.

Does the fellowship factor make a difference in your church and your life? I encourage you to ask the Lord, even this moment, to search your heart to help you determine the truth. If you are found lacking, seek to embrace a proper attitude toward the impaired.

Let us never forget, we have the Lord's strength and guidance to help shape us into the caring ministers Scripture commands us to be.

9 Facing Frustration, Bitterness, and Rejection

When confronted with severe impairments or afflictions, some are tempted to blame God for their troubles. As pressure mounts and difficulties increase, frustration may lead to blame, blame to resentment, resentment to apathy or bitterness toward the Lord.

Humanly speaking, even the best of us can find ourselves frustrated when faced with the trials and tragedies of life. For some, extended times of trouble may lead us to question and even deny God and His love for us. The apostle Peter publicly denied Christ three times. It took Christ's miraculous resurrection from the dead to cause Peter to return to the fold. The apostle Thomas had turned so far from Christ that when informed of the Lord's resurrection he proclaimed, "Unless I see in His hands the print of the nails, and put my finger into the print of the nails, and put my hand into His side, I will not believe" (John 20:25). It took a personal appearance from the Lord to force Thomas to believe. Job grew so frustrated with the trials he faced that when confronted by God, he was compelled to repent in "dust and ashes" (Job 42:6). Natural as it may be, resentment, bitterness, and rejection are an affront to God and have the potential to destroy our lives.

There are many reasons men become frustrated with God when faced with serious troubles. Let's take a look at several factors that may shape how we handle frustration brought on by impairments, afflictions, and suffering.

Ignorance

Most of the world suffers from an extreme case of ignorance as it relates to God and His Word. Many people are deficient in their understanding of Him because they live their lives in spiritual darkness. The Bible brings this out when it says in Ephesians 4:17-19:

> This I say, therefore, and testify in the Lord, that you should no longer walk as the rest of the Gentiles walk, in the futility of their mind, having their understanding darkened, being alienated from the life of God, because of the ignorance that is in them, because of the hardening of their heart.

The hardening mentioned here is a product of a sin nature. Because sin separates us from God, it also separates us from His truth, thereby holding us in a state of spiritual ignorance. Overcoming it demands far more than an advanced degree in theology. It requires a personal relationship with God and His Holy Spirit. In John 14:16-17, 26 the Bible says:

> He will give you another Helper, that He may abide with you forever—the Spirit of truth, whom the world cannot receive, because it neither sees Him nor knows Him . . . the Holy Spirit, whom the Father will send in My name, He will teach you all things.

Overcoming ignorance of God demands an internal spiritual awakening that establishes basic faith and understanding. One of the greatest examples of how quickly a person can pass from ignorance to understanding is seen in Luke 23:39-43. There a criminal went from total ignorance of Christ to calling on Him for spiritual deliverance. Jesus confirmed the depth of the man's enlightenment by saying in verse 43, "Assuredly, I say to you, today you will be with Me in Paradise."

The spiritual ignorance of one criminal condemned him to eternal separation from God, while the faith of the other, guaranteed him forgiveness and eternal fellowship with God.

When tribulation comes our way, blame, resentment, and bitterness are likely to follow if our heart's understanding of God and His ways is deficient.

Ownership

One of the greatest contributors to man's bitterness and rejection of God comes from his concept of personal ownership. When push comes to shove, many do not believe they are possessions of God. If they did, they would approach Him with greater respect, reliance, and humility. The Bible says in Deuteronomy 10:14, "Indeed heaven and the highest heavens belong to the Lord your God, also the earth with all that is in it."

In the book of Daniel it reminds us that it is "God who holds your breath in His hand and owns all your ways" (Daniel 5:23). When it comes to ownership, Scripture clearly teaches that all humans unconditionally belong to God. How we choose to approach the relationship is up to us.

Freeing ourselves from a contentious relationship with God demands that we humbly accept our rightful place before Him as servants and possessions of the Almighty. As we do, we will be more equipped to face the trials and difficulties the world has to offer.

Trust

For many people, affixing blame and embracing bitterness toward God find their essence in the inability to unconditionally entrust all aspects of their lives to Him.

The most basic form of trust in God finds its genesis in the recognition of His existence. The Bible says in Psalm 14:1, "The fool has said in his heart, 'There is no God.'" Scripture acknowledges that there are some who refuse to recognize God's existence regardless the signs or evidence. It views such people as fools, because from God's perspective they deny the undeniable.

Those who now refuse to recognize God's existence may have once acknowledged it. Sadly, when faced with tragedy or disappointment, restlessness may have led them to drift from God, and drifting may have led to apathy or even rejection of Him.

We see an example of this in the life of Charles Darwin, the father of the evolutionary theory. Early in life Charles was preparing to enter Christian ministry. As time passed, his recognition of God wavered. His father's death shook him to the point of condemning the doctrine of eternal punishment. In his autobiography Charles said:

> I can indeed hardly see how anyone ought to wish Christianity to be true; for if so the plain language of the text seems to show that the men who do not believe, and this would include my Father, Brother and almost all of my friends, will be everlasting punished. And this is a damnable doctrine.[1]

Darwin's view of God experienced an even greater blow when his favorite daughter, Annie, died of typhoid at the tender age of ten. "Annie's death marks the final destruction of Darwin's faith in a beneficent Christian God and a just moral universe."[2]

When God fails to meet our greatest expectations, apart from a firm and deeply grounded trust in Him, there is little to keep us from becoming bitter and inevitably rejecting Him. Humanly speaking, it is natural to reject someone who has greatly disappointed us.

Ultimately, bitterness toward God is rooted in an underlying distrust of Him. For Darwin the distrust slowly developed over many years, but it took the loss of his father and daughter to accentuate and expose it.

Charles Darwin, in some ways, is symbolic of millions of people just like him; people who at one point in their lives recognized God's existence, but in the end renounced Him due to some sort of tragic, life-changing event.

---

1. Charles Darwin, "The Autobiography of Charles Darwin," (1809-1882).
2. Janet Browne, *Charles Darwin: Voyaging*, (Princeton: Princeton University Press, 1995) pp. 498-504.

The essence of one's trust in God is truly put to the test when tragedy strikes. A relationship with God founded on anything less than a deep and profound trust in Him will fail to weather life's greatest storms.

Perspective

Another element that may lead some to become bitter toward God is their perspective of reality. Perspective denotes the actual or perceived vantage point from which one views a particular subject or event.

When confronted with a particular difficulty, some may be tempted to believe they have a superior vantage point to God's. Frustration and bitterness may set in if God "fails" to see things as they do. God's love, mercy, sympathy, and even His very existence may be questioned if He fails to perform as expected.

Regardless of man's perspective of reality, God's vantage point is all encompassing and unlimited in scope—man's is finite in every way. When faced with adversity, if our heart's desire is to overcome and glorify God, keeping things in godly perspective is necessary.

When God led Israel from captivity in Egypt, the people daily witnessed mighty miracles. No matter how many miracles they witnessed, it did not keep them from turning on God and His appointed leader, Moses (Exodus 15:24; 16:2; 17:3; 32:1; Numbers 14:2-4; 21:5). Why? Because at the moment of crisis they believed they understood the situation better than God. Israel was wrong and their misguided perspective did nothing to help them overcome their difficulties and worked to create a multitude of unnecessary hardships.

Forgetfulness

When serious trouble comes, it can produce a sort of emotional, psychological, and spiritual tunnel vision. It can cause some to block out all else, becoming overwhelmed with the difficulties at hand.

During these times, some are quick to forget the many ways God has blessed and cared for them. Every breath and heartbeat is a blessing of God. Food, clothing, and shelter are blessings as well. God continually blesses man, and man continually forgets the multitude of blessings God showers upon him daily.

In his selfishness, man demands bigger and better blessings daily, forgetting God owes him nothing. With such a selfish and self-centered approach to God's blessings, it's no wonder so many people become bitter when things don't go as desired.

When Darwin's daughter Annie died, God gave Charles the choice between focusing on the blessing or the loss. Charles, even in a state of mourning, could have praised God for the ten years of blessing with his daughter. Instead, he opted to forget the goodness of God and reject Him because of the loss.

Sadly, Darwin, like many others do, forgot that God did not have to give him one year of blessing, never mind ten. God did not promise us a loving wife, husband, child, family, or friend. Yet man holds God accountable for promises He never made.

God does not steal from man; man steals from God. Man steals from Him by withholding the honor, praise, thankfulness, and obedience He deserves. When God takes a life, He is not robbing man; He is claiming that which belongs to Him.

Darwin forgot that things such as family are nothing more than temporary gifts from God, not eternal chattel. For the true believer, a wife, a husband, a child, family, and friends at best are eternal brothers and sisters in Christ—not eternal possessions created for their pleasure.

God does not promise us eyes, ears, arms, and legs. He does not promise that we will never experience impairments, afflictions, or suffering in this world. Yet many arrogantly forget His blessings and thereby reject Him for promises He never made.

Betrayal

Those who consider themselves good and faithful followers of God, by virtue of their relationship with Him, may suppose He owes them special recognition and treatment. Humanly speaking, some believe the more good they do for God, the more favor they will receive. This false assumption may lead some to believe God has betrayed them when difficulties arise.

The apostle Paul did more for God than most people do in several lifetimes. What was God's response to Paul's exceptional commitment? In 2 Corinthians 12:7-9 Paul says:

> And lest I should be exalted above measure by the abundance of the revelations, a thorn in the flesh was given to me, a messenger of Satan to buffet me, lest I be exalted above measure. Concerning this thing I pleaded with the Lord three times that it might depart from me. And He said to me, "My grace is sufficient for you, for My strength is made perfect in weakness."

Rather than receiving special favor, Paul received a "thorn in the flesh" to help him remain humble.

In Matthew 5:45 Jesus reminds us that, "He makes His sun rise on the evil and on the good, and sends rain on the just and on the unjust." In this world, God blesses those who love and hate Him, those who believe and reject Him.

Paul says in Romans 2:11, "For there is no partiality with God." Given this, why would anyone believe they deserve special treatment from God? Like it or not, all are called to experience impairments, afflictions, and suffering of varying degree. All are called to lose loved ones. Earth is not heaven. Life, suffering, and death are a perpetual display of grace entwined with justice.

Simplicity

When faced with times of trouble, there are those who reject God by rejecting His Word. When informed that afflictions, suffering, and death are by-products of man's sin nature, some dismiss this biblical teaching as too simplistic. They reason that it simply can't be explained away so easily. They believe the level of pain and suffering in the world demands a more complex scenario.

When it comes to such things, how is it that people can ignore basic logic? Can one find a more profound explanation from evolution? Certainly not! Evolution offers an even more simplistic view of the origin of pain, suffering, and sin than that found in the Bible. Truth does not necessitate complexity. There are billions of very simple concepts representing various truths in the world.

On a cosmic scale, the sun emits an enormous amount of light every day. Regularly, solar light reaches the surface of the moon, reflects back into space, and travels toward the earth. Even though the feat is tremendous, the concept can easily be explained. The simplicity of the concept has no bearing on its validity.

Some people may yearn for a deeper, more complex reason for man's troubles, but the fact is, a simple answer does not alter the viability of a truth. A simple yet truthful answer must be viewed for what it is—simple truth. To do otherwise runs the risk of rejecting all truth merely because of its simplicity.

Other Potential Reasons

There are many other reasons people become frustrated and bitter with God. Additional reasons include personal arrogance ("God exists for me; I do not exist for Him"), irresponsibility (failure to recognize our role in averting trouble), self-preservation (favoring self above God), weakness (we have a shallow relationship with God), peer pressure ("My family and friends dishonor God; I will as well"), and hurt feelings ("I can't get over my disappointment with God for letting me down").

Dealing with Our Attitude

As we encounter life's difficulties, we can choose to rationalize our disappointment or recognize and confront it. To properly deal with our frustration, we must opt to address several important factors.

Our View of God

The first and most important step is to examine our view of God. How we view Him will in most cases dictate our response toward Him when faced with life-altering difficulties.

If we have not entered into a personal and committed relationship with God, on His terms, we are prime candidates to become bitter and to reject Him when distress comes our way.

How are we to view God? We are to see Him through the framework of absolute love. Deuteronomy 6:5 says, "You shall love the Lord your God with all your heart, with all your soul, and with all your strength." When we view God through this lens, it is impossible to become resentful toward Him.

A full and complete love for God is essential, but recognizing His position over us is important as well. Notice Deuteronomy 6:5 refers to God as Lord. The Lord is the Creator and Sustainer of man, and He deserves a respect characterized by awe and wonder over His majesty.

Deuteronomy 6:5 also uses the term *all* to describe the extent to which we are to offer ourselves up to Him—with all our heart, soul, and strength. Why does God expect all we have to offer? Simply put, because He deserves all. As creatures created by God, humans owe their very existence to Him. Man is born in debt to God.

Viewing God as we ought will help shape a proper attitude toward Him and sustain us during times of prosperity and misfortune.

Our Approach to Trouble

How we approach trouble will determine the level of negativity developed when we are engaged by it. If we approach such things like a victim, or with apathy, this will work to enhance the depth of negativity we develop.

Knowing who we are and where we are in Christ is essential to overcoming troubles. The goal is to overcome obstacles with God's aid, not in spite of it.

Becoming proactive rather than reactive will help us avoid needless frustration and bitterness when approaching times of trouble. Upon entering into a personal relationship with Christ, we must become grounded in the faith. Steps to becoming grounded include locating a solid Bible-believing church that preaches, teaches, and strives to practice God's Word. The church we go to is relevant because when it embraces it's calling, equipping leading to spiritual maturity will be rendered.

On a personal level, it is important that we strive to partake in a time of prayer and Bible study on a daily basis. Steps such as these will help us avoid spiritual failure and set us on the path to becoming like Christ.

Another important aspect is to strive to maintain a life of purity that is pleasing to God. When we sin, it is essential that we confess our sin to God, seek forgiveness, and turn from sin immediately. Purity maintains the lines of communication with God—sin breaks them down. Purity strengthens us for times of trouble—sin weakens us and creates vulnerability.

It is impossible to predict when trouble will come our way. Thus, preparing ourselves daily to more effectively deal with such things must be a top priority.

Our Lives

If a severe trouble enters your life, the natural reaction is to pull back from life and go into a shell. Initially, this may be necessary, but as time passes, it is essential to begin living life once again. Failure to do so will ruin your life and decrease your ability to embrace God's will for it.

Keep Things in Perspective

One of the most difficult yet helpful things we can do when faced with severe troubles is to keep things in perspective. Recognizing that things always could be worse is a helpful and realistic practice. For some the tendency is to fool themselves into believing that no one has experienced the level of suffering or trials they have. This simply is not the case. Many people have suffered greatly over the history of mankind. Life can always get worse.

Amid one of the greatest struggles of his life, the apostle Paul said in 2 Corinthians 1:8-11:

> For we do not want you to be ignorant, brethren, of our trouble which came to us in Asia: that we were burdened beyond measure, above strength, so that we despaired even of life. Yes, we had the sentence of death in ourselves, that we should not trust in ourselves but in God who raises the dead, who delivered us from so great a death, and does deliver us; in whom we trust that He will still deliver us.

Paul kept things in perspective during the most difficult of times. Even when he felt the presence of death all around him, he trusted in God.

When Paul found himself struggling for his life, surely Scriptures like Psalm 34:17-19 must have helped sustain him.

> The righteous cry out, and the Lord hears, and delivers them out of all their troubles. The Lord is near to those who have a broken heart, and saves such as have a contrite spirit. Many are the afflictions of the righteous, but the Lord delivers him out of them all.

As we work through the many struggles of life, like Paul, let us remember God cares and is attentive to our hurt.

Understanding the Ramifications

All of us at some point become frustrated and even bitter over the various trials and troubles we face. As with anything in life, negativity can produce unfruitful results when left to fester.

As time passes, frustration can morph into bitterness. The single most devastating by-product is its ability to separate us from the One most capable of helping us weather the storms–God.

As much as bitterness can separate us from God, it also works to create a sense of self-pity. The problem with allowing ourselves to lapse into self-pity is it robs us of the desire to keep on keeping on. Bitterness tends to warp our perspective of life, those who care about us, and the many opportunities God lays before us. It eventually implodes, driving us to a narrow inward focus rather than a broad outward one. Bitterness is like a deep pit that surrounds, controls, and keeps us from advancing and fulfilling all that God wants us to be.

Bitterness does not make things better; it only makes things worse. Excessive frustration, bitterness, and rejection of God never solve problems; they only create and extend them.

Understanding the Response

When faced with frustration, bitterness, and rejection, we can choose to embrace or deny such things. By embracing them, we allow them to rule over our lives. By denying their power over us, we free ourselves to begin the healing process and start moving on with our lives.

In Psalm 73:26 the psalmist said, "My flesh and my heart fail; but God is the strength of my heart and my portion forever." Even when sorrow strikes and the heart fails, God and the strength He offers will always be there for us.

Proverbs 3:5-6 says, "Trust in the Lord with all your heart, and lean not on your own understanding; in all your ways acknowledge Him, and He shall direct your paths." Trusting in God, allowing Him to lead and guide us, is the best response to deep frustration and bitterness. Humanly speaking, we may not always understand why things happen, we may not always like the way things are happening, but we can rest assured that God is in control and "all things work together for good to those who love God, to those who are the called according to His purpose" (Romans 8:28-29).

Few men or women have walked the jagged path of heartache and sorrow that John and Abigail Adams (second president of the United States and his wife, both devout Christians) did between the years of 1811 and 1813. During this trying period their son Thomas was nearly crippled for life, two of their grandchildren died, their widowed daughter-in-law Sally contracted tuberculosis and was in critical condition, their beloved brother-in-law Richard Cranch died of heart failure, and Abigail's sister Mary Cranch died of tuberculosis. One of John's closest friends from the Revolution, Benjamin Rush, suddenly died of typhus, and their beloved daughter, Nabby, died of breast cancer. John Adams himself was badly injured by tearing a gash in his leg to the bone, which confined him for months. As extensive as this list of tragedies is it could have contained additional trials unique to that day and age.

In a letter to her son John Quincy, Abigail said, "Heaven be praised your father and I have been supported through all this solemn scene with fortitude and I hope Christian resignation."[3] She later mentioned to John Quincy regarding his father, "Bowed

---

3. David McCullough, *John Adams* (Simon & Schuster, 2001) p. 614.

down as he has been . . . he has not sunk under it."[4] In correspondence with Thomas Jefferson, John Adams noted, "The love of God and His creation, delight, joy, triumph, exultation in my own existence . . . are my religion."[5]

As Christians, John and Abigail had been shaken by this heavy, relentless time of physical and emotional pain, but both overcame any desire to grow bitter toward God and reject Him. They overcame by maintaining a proper view of God and a proper approach to trouble, and continuing to live their lives while keeping things in perspective.

With few of the comforts of life, these early American believers overcame some of the most difficult trials life has to offer. John and Abigail understood the meaning of "Trust in the Lord with all your heart, and lean not on your own understanding" (Proverbs 3:5). They suffered and experienced extended times of mourning over their many losses, but in the end both embraced victory over their struggles. Just as John and Abigail conquered their trials, let us learn from their example and do likewise!

---

4. Ibid., p. 614.
5. Ibid., p. 614.

10 A Tribute To The Triumphant

Throughout the world there are scores of godly people struggling with various types of physical impairments. Many of them, through the empowering of the Holy Spirit, are having an important impact on their communities, neighborhoods, churches, and families. Joni Eareckson Tada, for example, has had a global impact through film, music recordings, and books. Through her ministry many have been encouraged and challenged in their walk with Jesus Christ. Because of her wonderful example, even those with severe impairments find hope and have come to realize they too may have a role in the Lord's work.

As special as Joni is, there are countless other physically impaired Christians ministering on Christ's behalf. Let's take a brief look at a small handful of people who have bravely sought to serve Christ in spite of their impairments.

The Triumph of Anna Ladman

Every Christian who struggles with a physical impairment, and daily overcomes to the glory of God, is a special and courageous person. Yet as we consider the circumstances surrounding each of these people, we realize some have faced greater trials than others. One such person is a Ukrainian woman named Anna Ladman.

Anna was born in 1936 into a Christian family. During her years at home, Anna was taught the Bible and eventually accepted Jesus as her Savior. Sadly, she became interested in a young man who was not a Christian, and later she agreed to marriage.

From the beginning, their marriage was a rough and rocky one. As time passed, to her dismay, Anna realized her husband had no interest in Christianity. Worse yet, he was plagued with some sort of psychological disorder.

Problems such as these robbed her life of hope and happiness. Yet within the confines of her emotional prison, Anna found comfort and strength through her relationship with Christ.

Just when life appeared to be near hopeless, the Lord provided a ray of sunshine in Anna's life through the birth of a son. As with all Christian mothers, she entrusted her little boy to the Lord and prayed that one day he would come to Christ.

As the years passed, Anna began to wonder if her son would ever accept Christ. Even though she attempted to guide him to the Lord, her efforts seemed useless because he had no interest in Christianity. This upset Anna so much that one day while praying she told the Lord she was prepared to give up her life to see her son become a Christian.

Nothing seemed to be going right for Anna. Her relationship with her husband was sour. Her son continued to show no interest in Christianity. Humanly speaking, could things get any worse? They most certainly could. Unknowingly, Anna stood on the threshold of the most horrible and ghastly experience one could imagine.

One day shortly after arriving home, Anna was confronted by the sight of her troubled husband viciously lunging at her with axe in hand. A struggle ensued, and she bravely withstood his violent attacks. Because of the intensity of his relentless challenge, she soon became fatigued. As her strength failed, it was just a matter of time before the axe brutally struck her head and arms.

After the beating, Anna was taken to the hospital. Seeing no way to save Anna's badly mutilated arms, the doctors amputated them above the elbows.

After suffering this great evil at the hands of her husband, Anna longed to die. She could not help but think that a woman with no arms was useless. But as evil a curse as Anna had suffered, the Lord would not allow her to die, for through this curse He would provide a wonderful blessing.

It all started when some young Christians began visiting her during her time of trial. While at her home they would sing and talk about Jesus and the Bible. These young ministers not only caught Anna's ear, but her son's as well. Because of their loving ministry to Anna, her son accepted the Lord.

After Anna's son came to Christ, she realized the Lord had used the curse of her impairment as a means of blessing her son with salvation. As a result, she turned to God and asked forgiveness for all the bitterness she had stored up. As Anna surrendered her dreadful situation to the Lord, He graciously revived her sense of hope and joy. He added to her revival by enabling Anna and her son to invent special devices that would act as artificial limbs.

The Lord also blessed Anna in another way through her physical impairment. Prior to the loss of her arms, Anna's ministry to others was limited, but because of her impairment, her sphere of ministry was greatly increased. All of a sudden, people who had lost their arms were writing and visiting her in hopes of gaining advice on how to deal with their loss. Anna, who once believed herself to be totally useless and fit for death, became very useful in the hands of God.

From the ashes of tragedy and despair, the Lord took a broken woman and blessed her many times over. To His glory, the Lord has taken a once-unknown woman and used her life to challenge and encourage others around the world.

The Triumph of Pastor Larry Ott

Have you ever heard someone say, "I don't go lookin' for trouble; trouble comes lookin' for me"? To some degree this describes a monumental moment in the life of Pastor Larry Ott.

At the tender age of six, Larry and his sister were struck with polio. For reasons only known to God, his sister recovered with the exception of a limp. Larry, on the other hand, was left paralyzed in both legs and an arm that continued to deteriorate.

As one might expect, while growing up, Larry struggled with the fact that he was severely impaired. At a time when other children were running, jumping and riding bicycles, all he could do was dream of such things. At times, Larry's remorse was so great that at night, with heart in hand, young Larry would cry out to God, "Heal me and I will be a missionary. I will even go to Africa!" At times like these, often the only response the Lord may have for young and old alike is, "Beloved, be still and know that I am God."

During his time of soul-searching and wrestling with the reality God had set before him, Larry was challenged by the Lord's response to the apostle Paul when he too struggled with a "thorn." For Larry the pinnacle of his struggle came when faced with doing as God desired or as he desired. After much turmoil, he humbled his heart and fully embraced the Lord's will. With this decision came something Larry had never fully experienced—true peace within.

By surrendering his will to God, Larry no longer saw his physical impairment as a handicap, but as a tool. In an article Larry said:

> Since I have accepted myself, as God intended, I have the freedom to pursue His purposes for my life. I realize my disability is the greatest tool I have in my ministry. It allows me to sympathize, understand, and feel the heart of those God has entrusted me with.[1]

Pastor Larry Ott, a man of God who looked his "demon" squarely in the eye and, rather than humble himself to it, humbled himself to God. Rather than cursing God because of his impairment, he now thanks the Lord for it. Instead of being bitter, he has found peace. Praise be to God for Pastor Larry and all the Lord has accomplished in and through his life!

---

1. Larry Ott, *Opening a Closed Room*, pp. 15-16.

The Triumph of Gianna Jessen

Have you ever played a word-association game, where someone says a word and you're supposed to say the first thing that comes to mind? If I were playing that game and someone said the word *abortion*, the first word that would come to my mind is *sin*. Why? Because abortion usurps the life of the unborn and renders it helpless in the hands of another. Under certain circumstances God allows the taking of a life (capital punishment, self-defense, accidental death, etc.), abortion is not one of them (Exodus 20:13; Genesis 9:5; Numbers 35:9-28, 30-31; Romans 13:4).

Gianna Jessen is living proof of just how evil abortion is. On April 6, 1977, Gianna's biological mother enrolled in an abortion clinic to receive a saline injection. The procedure was meant to kill the baby and thus terminate the young woman's seven-month pregnancy. But on this particular day things did not go as planned. For some reason, after the deadly chemical was injected into the womb, the baby survived. Though baby Gianna did not realize it at the time, through her birth she had triumphed over evil forces—forces that in the name of freedom encouraged her near demise!

The typically fatal procedure backfired. Instead of bringing death, the saline injection brought disability. The tiny legs of this young warrior had been badly damaged by cerebral palsy. This terrible affliction led doctors to predict that Gianna would never walk or even sit up.

Through the loving nurture of her foster mother, Penny, and her adopted mother, Diana, several surgeries, a great deal of pain and suffering, and a strong will to succeed, Gianna overcame her second great obstacle and is now able to walk.

Only one major barrier remained in Gianna's life, and that was forgiving her biological mother for attempting to abort her. This remarkable victory took place not long after she learned of the attempted abortion.

Of the many struggles and victories she has experienced, forgiveness stands high above the rest. Humanly speaking, few could condemn the broken heart of a child for failing to mend. Yet as Gianna herself notes, forgiveness was possible due to God's grace.

Through the great tragedy Gianna endured, she is now able to share her story with others. Because of Gianna, people are able to see the "other side" of abortion. As someone who survived the holocaustic influence of abortion, Gianna has helped many women who aborted their babies to find peace with themselves.

When one contemplates all Gianna has been able to accomplish in such a short period of time, one might wonder how much talent has been extinguished as a result of abortion. How many great poets, authors, singers, athletes, scientists, explorers, and leaders will never be? It's a sad thought, but Gianna's triumph challenges us to consider this woeful situation.

The Triumph of Wayne Davidson

When I think of Christians who have struggled with and overcome their physical impairments to God's glory, one person who comes to mind is Wayne Davidson. I met Wayne while attending seminary. He worked as the school's comptroller and on occasion exercised his preaching skills during chapel services.

When Wayne was twenty-one months old, he contracted polio. This terrible disease attacked and deformed his feet, legs, and back. To this day he suffers from the scars of his childhood illness.

One of the most impressive things about Wayne is his drive to succeed. With a bachelor's degree from Rutgers University, a Master of Divinity degree from Biblical Theological Seminary, a position as comptroller of a distinguished school, and a solid reputation as a husband and father, Wayne has boldly persevered and moved forward.

His example and accomplishments broadcast the fact that just because someone is physically impaired, that does not mean he is intellectually, emotionally, spiritually, or vocationally impaired.

One of the most memorable moments of my time in seminary was when Wayne shared a message during a chapel service. In that message he openly and honestly shared some of his innermost and personal feelings.

That morning, Wayne spoke of God's unconditional love for us. To help us better understand its relevance, he told of a lesson he learned through his wife. At one time in his life he firmly believed he might never get married. He felt it impossible for any woman to look beyond his bodily disfigurement.

This theory began to change when he met his future wife. As their relationship grew, so did their love and respect for each other. By expressing a full measure of unconditional love and acceptance, his wife taught him about God in a way no theology class could ever have done.

Through this simple yet effective lesson, we learn that regardless of a man's physical prowess, before God all of us are born spiritually deformed in one way or another. Yet through the blood of Jesus Christ, God no longer sees us as spiritually deformed, but as whole, sound, and attractive to the eye. Through the blood of Christ we have been created anew!

Those who may be struggling with the same thoughts Wayne once did can embrace the lesson he learned. The joy and happiness God freely showered upon him can bathe your life as well. But before this can take place, you must surrender all before the throne of God. As you align yourself with His revealed will, be prepared to accept it as the bottom line. When you do so, like Wayne, you too will taste of the fruits of triumph.

The Triumph of the Physically Impaired

Through the lives of these people, we can see how important the physically impaired are. Anna, Larry, Gianna and Wayne have taught and exemplify the meaning of forgiveness, love, and perseverance. Through their lives we can see that the physically impaired are greatly needed and have much to offer.

Let us never forget, the physically impaired are people created in God's image, not defective animals. As a result, the Lord extends His hand of eternal fellowship to them through Christ's death and resurrection. And with this gift, they can triumph, not only in life, but in death as well.

May the church of Jesus Christ be mindful of the words of the Lord when He said, "Whatever you did for one of the least of these brothers of Mine, you did for Me" (Matthew 25:40). As the physically impaired triumph over their spiritual impairment, they are welcomed by God into His eternal fellowship. They deserve to be welcomed into His church as well. We must strive to love and serve them, and provide opportunities for them to grow and serve the local church. In doing so, together we will "fight the good fight of the faith" (1 Timothy 6:12) to the honor and glory of our Lord and Savior, Jesus Christ.

Small Group Study Questions
Chapter 1 - Identity Lost

The goal of this section is to encourage thoughtful discussion as it relates to the subject of Identity Lost. To get the most out of this section, group members should freely and openly share their understanding and personal feelings regarding the subjects discussed.

1. How well do you relate with those who are physically impaired?

2. What do you feel you and others could do to better empathize with the physically impaired?

3. What makes the physically impaired special people?

4. Is there a physically impaired person whose example has helped you in some way? Please explain how.

5. When you read The Handicap Plea, what do you feel? After reading it, will you treat the physically impaired differently?

6. Do you agree with Chuck Colson's observation about America? Why or why not?

7. Do you believe you are a magnificent mammal or magnificent man? Why?

8. Does it really make a difference whether man was created in God's image? Why?

9. Do you believe older people who are ill should be "humanely" put to sleep?

Small Group Study Questions
Chapter 2 - Who Sinned?

The goal of this section is to encourage thoughtful discussion as it relates to the subject of Who Sinned? To get the most out of this section, group members should freely and openly share their understanding and personal feelings regarding the subjects discussed.

1. There are five potential avenues that may bring about physical impairments and afflictions. What are they?

2. On a personal level, what can we do to discourage needless impairments and afflictions from occurring?

3. What was the purpose behind the blind man's impairment?

4. If Jesus told you that your impairment was present that the "work of God might be displayed" in your life, how would you respond?

5. Does it help to know that your impairments are a result of our predecessor Adam? Why?

6. Are you a true Patron of God? If so, what do you base your patronage on? (Being a good person, you're a hard worker, a relationship with Jesus Christ, etc.).

7. What is the significance of Christ's message regarding the Galileans and the eighteen who died when the tower in Siloam fell on them?

8. What are you placing your trust in? The things of this world or Christ? Why have you placed your trust in one or the other?

Small Group Study Questions
Chapter 3 - The Thorn

The goal of this section is to encourage thoughtful discussion as it relates to the subject of The Thorn. To get the most out of this section, group members should freely and openly share their understanding and personal feelings regarding the subjects discussed.

1. From a biblical perspective, what are the five purposes physical impairments serve?

2. Why does God use physical impairments to enforce His commandments?

3. If someone acts foolishly and hurts themselves as a result, should God be blamed for not overriding the person's decision?

4. In what ways is God showing equality through physical impairments?

5. Can we actually grow as people as a result of physical impairments?

6. What sort of benefits might a person derive from a physical impairment?

7. Who is exalted by a physical impairment?

8. Even as painful and life-changing as a physical impairment may be, do you believe it can serve a positive purpose? Why or why not?

Small Group Study Questions
Chapter 4 - The Burdens

The goal of this section is to encourage thoughtful discussion as it relates to the subject of The Burdens. To get the most out of this section, group members should freely and openly share their understanding and personal feelings regarding the subjects discussed.

1. How important is the presence of the physically impaired as it relates to Scripture?

2. What is the difference between induced and uninduced impairments or afflictions? What about the literal use from the figurative?

3. As you read through this chapter, what physical impairments stood out most to you?

4. How do you feel about God using physical impairments or afflictions as tools in establishing His purposes for man?

5. Does God really care about the physically impaired? If so, what did you learn in this chapter that would lead you to this understanding?

6. What was God's purpose for including the physically impaired and their burdens in the Bible?

Small Group Study Questions
Chapter 5 - The Agony of Victory

The goal of this section is to encourage thoughtful discussion as it relates to the subject of The Agony of Victory. To get the most out of this section, group members should freely and openly share their understanding and personal feelings regarding the subjects discussed.

1. Do you believe all men are born into this world spiritually impaired? If not, why?

2. What are some of the evils that have resulted due to man's spiritual impairment?

3. What were the three things mentioned that went into the Physician's treatment?

4. Were you aware of just how much suffering Jesus experienced to pay the price for man's sin?

5. Which element of His suffering do you personally feel was the worse?

6. Through His suffering and death Jesus accomplished a great deal. What do you believe was the most significant result of Jesus' ministry?

7. If you are physically impaired and are a true follower of Christ, how do you feel about your future resurrection body?

Small Group Study Questions
Chapter 6 - The Calling

The goal of this section is to encourage thoughtful discussion as it relates to the subject of The Calling. To get the most out of this section, group members should freely and openly share their understanding and personal feelings regarding the subjects discussed.

1. Please describe the concept of "putting off the old self."

2. Prior to engaging in the process of "putting off," what must first happen to us?

3. Are there many ways to establish a relationship with God? Please explain your response.

4. How did you understand the meaning of "spiritual therapy"?

5. What does it mean to "put on the new self"?

6. What is the first and most important thing we must "put on"?

7. What are some other important things we must "put on" or "clothe" ourselves with?

8. When seeking to prepare ourselves, what are three very important things we must do?

9. What is the primary goal of the believer's calling?

Small Group Study Questions
Chapter 7 - The Comforter's Care

The goal of this section is to encourage thoughtful discussion as it relates to the subject of The Comforter's Care. To get the most out of this section, group members should freely and openly share their understanding and personal feelings regarding the subjects discussed.

1. Who is the Comforter spoken of in this chapter?

2. How does it make you feel (if you are a true believer in Christ) knowing that the Holy Spirit resides within you?

3. Given the fact that the Comforter equally indwells all true believers, does this have any impact on how others should view the importance of the physically impaired?

4. Why do you believe the Comforter treats the impaired the same as the non-impaired?

5. What are the main ways in which the Comforter cares for all of God's children?

6. What are three important functions the Comforter plays in the life of the impaired who are Christians?

7. Contrast the benefits between Christians and non-Christians who are physically impaired. Approach this question from the perspective that believers have the Comforter and non-believers do not.

Small Group Study Questions
Chapter 8 - The Fellowship Factor

The goal of this section is to encourage thoughtful discussion as it relates to the subject of The Fellowship Factor. To get the most out of this section, group members should freely and openly share their understanding and personal feelings regarding the subjects discussed.

1. Why do you believe Christ included those who are "sick" in His message regarding the coming judgment in Matthew 25:31-40.

2. In your opinion how important is the Fellowship Factor to the emotional and spiritual success of those who are physically impaired?

3. How do you feel about barriers such as stigmatization, generalizations, limitations, etc. Are they acceptable within the true church?

4. From your perspective what can be done to help others, both impaired and unimpaired, deal with and overcome such barriers?

5. If you are not physically impaired, how would you feel if the church treated you as a guest rather than as family? Explain why you would respond in such a manner.

6. After reading this chapter do you see the importance of such things as building accessibility, temperature, various impediments, structural stability, etc. in a different light?

7. Are there any additional avenues you or your church could put into practice?

Small Group Study Questions
Chapter 9 - Facing Frustration

The goal of this section is to encourage thoughtful discussion as it relates to the subject of Facing Frustration, Bitterness, and Rejection. To get the most out of this section, group members should freely and openly share their understanding and personal feelings regarding the subjects discussed.

1. What personal trial frustrated you the most?

2. Are you surprised that great men of God such as Job, Peter and Thomas became frustrated?

3. What is your typical response to frustrating experiences?

4. There are several factors that may shape how you handle frustration. What are they?

5. How important is our attitude when we encounter times of trials and frustration?

6. Does our view of God impact how we treat Him when we encounter times of trouble and frustration?

7. By keeping things in perspective, can it really help us deal with troubles and frustration?

8. What are some of the ramifications that may occur when we become frustrated?

9. How should we respond to times of trouble and frustration? How was it possible for John and Abigail Adams to handle so many difficulties in such a short period of time?

Small Group Study Questions
Chapter 10 - A Tribute To The Triumphant

The goal of this section is to encourage thoughtful discussion as it relates to the subject of A Tribute To The Triumphant. To get the most out of this section, group members should freely and openly share their understanding and personal feelings regarding the subjects discussed.

1. What grabbed you the most about each of these people?

2. What elements within their lives cause each of these people to stand out from others?

3. What do you believe was the motivating factor in each of their lives that helped them to triumph?

4. Do you find people such as this to be an encouragement to you as you face the struggles of life?

5. Why is it essential to have role models such as these?

6. What can each of us learn from their examples?

Helpful Organizations and Agencies

The list of organizations and agencies below is provided as a starting point for those in need of specific information. Inclusion in the list should not be viewed as an endorsement.

GENERAL DISABILITY

Disability Rights Education
Defense Fund
2212 Sixth Street
Berkeley, CA 94710
Telephone: 510.644.2555
Internet: dredf.org

Joni and Friends
P.O. Box 3333
Agoura Hills, CA 91376
Telephone: 818.707.5664
Internet: joniandfriends.org

National Council on Disability
1331 F Street, NW,
Suite 850
Washington, DC 20004
Telephone: 202.272.2004
Internet: ncd.gov

U.S. Department of Education
National Institute on Disability &
Rehabilitation Research
400 Maryland Avenue SW
Washington, DC 20202
Telephone: 800.872.5327

U.S. Department of Labor
Office of Disability
Employment Policy
Frances Perkins Building
200 Constitution Avenue, NW
Washington, DC 20210
Telephone: 866.633.7365
Internet: dol.gov/odep/

Patient Advocate Foundation
700 Thimble Shoals Blvd,
Suite 200
Newport News, VA 23606
Telephone: 800.532.5274

Physicians' Disability
Services, Inc.
P.O. Box 822
Severna Park, MD 21146
Telephone: 410.431.5279
Internet: disabilityfacts.com

US Architectural &Transportation Barriers Compliance Board
1331 F Street NW, Suite 1000
Washington, DC 20004
Telephone: 800.872.2253
Internet: access-board.gov

AMPUTEE

American Academy of
Orthotists & Prosthetists
526 King Street, Suite 201
Alexandria, VA 22314
Telephone 703.836.0788
Internet: oandp.org

American Amputee Foundation
P.O. Box 250218
Hillcrest Station
Little Rock, AR 72225
Telephone: 501.666.2523

AMPUTEE Continued

Amputee Coalition of America
900 East Hill Avenue, Suite 285
Knoxville, TN 37915
Telephone: 888.267.5669
Internet: amputee-coalition.org

Amputee Resource
Foundation of America, Inc.
2324 Wildwood Trail, Suite F104
Minnetonka, MN 55305
Internet: amputeeresource.org

National Amputation Foundation
40 Church Street
Malverne, NY 11565
Telephone: 516.887.3600
Internet: nationalamputation.org

AUTISM

Autism Society of America
7910 Woodmont Avenue,
Suite 300
Bethesda, MD 20814
Telephone: 800.328.8476
Internet: autism-society.org

BLINDNESS

American Council of the Blind
1155 15th Street NW, Suite 1004
Washington, DC 20005
Telephone: 800.424.8666
Internet: acb.org

American Foundation
for the Blind
11 Penn Plaza, Suite 300
New York, NY 10001
Telephone: 800.232.5463
Internet: afb.org

Bibles for the Blind and Visually
Handicapped International
3228 E. Rosehill Avenue
Terre Haute, IN 47805
Telephone: 812.466.4899
Internet: biblesfortheblind.org

Christian Record Services
P.O. Box 6097
Lincoln, NE 68506
Telephone: 402.488.0981

National Federation of the Blind
1800 Johnson Street
Baltimore, MD 21230
Telephone: 410.659.9314
Internet: nfb.org

National Library Service
for the Blind and
Physically Handicapped
1291 Taylor Street, NW
Washington, DC 20011
Telephone: 800.424.8567
Internet: loc.gov/nls

BRAIN INJURY

Brain Injury Association
8201 Greensboro Dr., Suite 611
McLean, VA 22102
Telephone: 800.444.6443
Internet: biausa.org

CANCER

American Cancer Society, Inc.
1599 Clifton Road NE
Atlanta, GA 30329
Telephone: 800.227.2345
Internet: cancer.org

CANCER continued

Cancer Care, Inc
275 7th Avenue
New York, NY 10001
Telephone: 800.813.4673
Internet: cancercare.org

Cancer Connection, Inc.
P.O. Box 60452
Florence, MA 01062
Telephone: 413.586.1642
Internet: cancer-connection.com

National Cancer Institute
Public Inquiries Office
6116 Executive Boulevard
Room 3036A
Bethesda, MD 20892
Telephone: 800.422.6237
Internet: nci.nih.gov

Leukemia and
Lymphoma Society
1311 Mamaroneck Avenue
White Plains, NY 10605
Telephone: 800.955.4572
Internet: leukemia-lymphoma.org

DEAFNESS

National Association of the Deaf
814 Thayer Avenue
Silver Spring, MD 20910
Telephone: 301.587.1788

MULTIPLE SCLEROSIS

The Multiple Sclerosis
Association of America
706 Haddonfield Road
Cherry Hill, NJ 08002
Telephone: 856.488.4500
Internet: msaa.com

Multiple Sclerosis Foundation
6350 North Andrews Avenue
Fort Lauderdale, FL 33309
Telephone: 888.673.6287
Internet: msfacts.org

NERVE DISORDERS

National Institute of Neurological Disorders and Stroke
P.O. Box 5801
Bethesda, MD 20824
Telephone: 800.352.9424
Internet: ninds.nih.gov

PARALYZATION

American Spinal
Injury Association
2020 Peachtree Road, NW
Atlanta, GA 30309
Telephone: 404.355.9772
Internet: asia-spinalinjury.org

Foundation for Spinal Cord Injury
Prevention, Care & Cure
11230 White Lake Road
Fenton, MI 48430
Telephone: 800.342.0330
Internet: fscip.org

National Spinal Cord
Injury Association
6701 Democracy Blvd.,
Suite 300-9
Bethesda, MD 20817
Telephone: 800.962.9629
Internet: spinalcord.org

Paralyzed Veterans of America
801 Eighteenth Street NW
Washington, DC 20006
Telephone: 800.424.8200
Internet: pva.org

Scripture Index of Passages Used

Reference	Page	Reference	Page
Genesis 1:26-27	16	Numbers 12:10	60
2:7, 21-22	17	12:11	25
2:16-17	29	14:2-4	126
3:17-19	28	21:5	126
9:5	139	21:7	62
11:30	58	35:9-28, 30-31	139
13:24	58	Deuteronomy 6:5	129, 130
17:9-14, 11, 12, 14	59	7:14	58
18:10	58	10:14	124
19:11	52	16:19	51
25:21	58	24:8	60
27:1	52	27:18	53
27:27-29	58	28:22	62
29:31	58	28:27	60
32:24-31	56	28:28	63
32:25	59	Judges 1:6	57
41:41-45	58	13:2-3	58
Exodus 4:1, 3, 6	60	16:4, 17, 19, 21	24
6:30	59	1 Samuel 1:5, 20	58
15:24	126	3:2	52
16:2	126	3:20	58
17:3	126	4:18	56
20:13	139	13:14	27
20:14	23	15:22	37
32:1	126	20:14-15, 16, 42	56
15:24	126	21:10-15	62
Leviticus 1:1-17	69	28	96
4:1-5, 19	69	2 Samuel 4:4	56
7:1-7, 16	69	9:1-13, 11	56
12-15	59	11:5, 27	27
13-14	60	12:13, 14, 16	27
13:40	59	1 Kings 13:4	25
18:6	26	13:6	25
18:20-23	23	14:4	52
19:14	55	15:23	62
19:18	82	2 Kings 2:19	57
20:10-16	23	5:1, 27	60
20:20-21	57	6:18	52
21:18-19	56, 57	7:3	60
Numbers 5:2-4	60	2 Kings 15:5	60
5:21	62	1 Chronicles 28:9	89

Scripture Index of Passages Used / 157

2 Chronicles 16:12	62	Ezekiel 3:26	54
21:15-19	62	7:17	59
Job 2:4-5, 7	30	24:27	54
2:7, 9, 10	31, 60	Daniel 4:30	63
4:14	59	5:23	124
31:22	56	10:15	53
Job 38:15	56	Nahum 3:19	62
39:6	57	Habakkuk 2:19	54
42:6	122	3:16	62
Psalm 14:1	44	Matthew 4:24	63, 115
34:17-19	131	5:28	65
38:8	59	5:44, 45	40, 58
38:13	53	5:45	128
38:13-14	54	7:12	107
39:1-2	53	8:2	60
49:14	64	9:2	61
51:5	23, 91	11:5	56
51:11	89	11:27	69
58:3	23	12:36	65
58:4	53	15:14	51
73:26	132	15:30-31	56, 57
119:54-55, 144	84	16:21	66
127:3-5	57	16:22, 23	67
Proverbs 3:5	134	17:15	63
3:5-6	133	20:17-19	66
3:11-12	38	21:14	56
25:19	56	22:39	107
26:7	55	23:16	51
26:18	63	25:21	47
28.9	37	25:31-40	101
Ecclesiastes 4:9-10	100	25:40	141
Isaiah 1:6	62	27:46	68
32:4	59	28:18-20	85, 114
42:19	53	Mark 3:1	56
53:7	54	7:31-37	54
59:2	91	9:14-28, 17, 25, 26	54
63:10	88	9:43	57
64:6	65	10:46, 51-52	52
Jeremiah 6:10	59	Luke 1:7, 57	58
17:5	89	1:19-22	54
17:10	89	1:20	55
23:9	59	4:1-12	67
30:12	62	5:18, 18-26	61
Lamentations 4:8	56	5:31-32	66

Luke 6:6	56	Romans 1:4	79
7:22	54	1:17	80
8:43	62	2:11	128
13:1, 2-5	32	3:23	65, 70, 91
14:2	62	3:25-26	69, 78, 80
14:13	57	5:1	80
15:4-6	102	5:6-11	78
17:12	60	5:12	28, 64
18:33	70	6:21	24
22:42, 44	67	6:23	65, 78
23:39-43	123	8:5	77
John 1:45	84	8:14	96
3:3	91	8:16	88
9:1-12	52	8:16-17	72
9:2	26	8:26-27	97
9:2-3	23	8:28-29	133
9:3	28	10:9-11	78
10:10	84	11:25	51
14:2-3	72	12:13	102
14:15	37	13:4	139
14:17, 18	90	13:12	81
14:16-17, 26	124	13:14	79
14:26	87, 88	14:10-11	44
15:26	88	15:5-6	121
16:8-11	88, 90	1 Corinthians 2:10	88
16:13	96	2:13	95
16:13-14	95	6:19	88
20:19	88	11:27-32	36
20:25	122	11:28	37
Acts 2:2-4	87	12:2	54
3:1-10, 2-3, 6, 7	55	12:11	88
3:10	56	12:26	102
8:32	54	13:1-3	81
9:8-9	52	15:26	64, 99
9:18	53	15:54-57	71
9:33	61	2 Corinthians 1:8-11	131
10:34-35	97	1:9	99
12:22	39	1:22, 24	80
12:23	62	3:14	51
14:8-10	56	4:12	47, 99
15:8	80	4:16-17	47
16:7	88	5:7	34
26:23	79	5:17	75, 92
28:8	62	5:18-21	69

2 Corinthians 9:13	102	1 Peter 5:8	81
12:7-9	127	2 Peter 1:8	57
12:7-10	41	1:9	51
12:8	42	1 John 2:18	95
12:9	43, 47	2:22	95
12:10	44, 45, 47	2:27	95
Galatians 3:27	79	3:3	37, 75
5:16, 16-17	94	4:8	38
5:19-21	77	4:19	79
6:6	102	5:4	71
6:7	25	5:11-13	89
6:7-8	39	5:13	71
6:8	71	Revelation 1:5	79
Ephesians 1:13-14	89	2:7	88
2:4-5	92	2:23	89
2:8-10	65, 85	20:15	65
2:8-10	78		
4:11-13	115		
4:17-19	123		
4:22-24	75, 93		
4:24	78, 85		
4:30	88, 89		
5:18	24, 26, 94		
5:23	79		
6:11-18	81		
Philippians 1:21	73		
3:20-21	73		
4:4	102		
Colossians 3:12	82		
1 Thessalonians 5:8	79		
1 Timothy 3:1-13	116		
5:23	61		
6:12	142		
2 Timothy 2:17	62		
3:16-17	83		
Titus 1:5-9	116		
Hebrews 3:13	114		
4:15	112		
10:25	114		
11:6	80		
11:35, 36-38	47		
12:11	38		
12:12-13	55		
13:16	102		

Subject Index
of Terms Used

Abortion, 13, 19, 26, 65, 139-140
Accountable, 39-40, 65, 109, 127
Accountability, 17, 33, 37, 44
Afflicted, 8, 25, 30, 31, 44, 47, 59, 61, 64, 66, 115
Affliction, 22-23, 25, 31, 32, 35, 37-47, 50, 57, 63-65, 70, 73, 77, 101, 122-123, 127-128, 132, 139, 144, 146
Ailments, 50, 59, 60-62, 101
Attack, 136
Attitude, 12, 40, 82, 121, 129-130, 151
Blind, 9, 11, 23, 28-29, 48, 52-53, 55, 63, 102, 113, 144
Blindness, 26, 28-29, 51-53, 55
Bitter, 111, 125-127, 129, 132, 134, 138
Bitterness, 48, 122, 124-126, 128, 130, 132-134, 137, 151
Care, 43, 53, 55, 64, 66, 82, 87, 89-91, 93, 95, 97, 100, 102, 108, 111-112, 118-119, 132, 146, 149
Caring, 7, 92, 100-102, 121
Christ, 10, 33, 36, 41, 43-48, 52-53, 57, 61, 63, 66-80, 82-89, 92-95, 97-101, 103-105, 113-115, 117, 119, 121-123, 127, 130, 135-137, 141-142, 144, 147, 149-150
Church, 36, 52, 55, 72, 79, 82, 95, 99, 102-110, 114-121, 130, 135, 141, 150
Comfort, 99, 121, 134, 136
Concern, 7, 43, 62, 82, 103, 105, 107, 110-112, 117, 121
Confront, 27, 38, 129
Creation, 17, 75, 92, 134
Creature, 17, 19, 74, 92, 130
Cry, 30, 68, 132, 138
Crying, 26, 31, 67, 104
Curse, 9, 28-31, 41, 55, 64, 72-73, 137
Cursed, 28, 53, 89
Deaf, 9, 11, 54-55, 63, 120
Deafness, 53-54
Death, 8, 19, 21, 23, 28-29, 32, 36-37, 39, 45, 56, 62, 64-65, 68-73, 75, 91-92, 97, 125, 128, 131-132, 137, 139, 141, 147
Devil, 30-31, 67, 81
Disabled, 18-19
Disability, 19, 28, 89, 138-139
Disfavor, 53, 57-58
Die, 27, 31, 36, 45, 64, 73, 137
Drugs, 18, 24, 26, 65
Dumb, 54, 63
Dying, 32
Encourage, 16, 21, 25, 27, 37, 39, 42, 44, 53, 77, 82, 90, 94, 96, 104-105, 107, 114, 116-119, 121, 137, 143-152
Encouragement, 9, 12, 37, 114-116, 118, 152
Euthanasia, 13, 19
Evil, 27-28, 40-41, 52, 54, 79, 81, 86, 128, 137, 139, 147
Evolution, 13-16, 128
Evolutionism, 16, 18
Evolve, 17, 20
Favor, 16, 39, 58, 76, 127-128
Fear, 9, 55, 87, 89, 97-98, 105, 111
Fearful, 89
Frail, 32, 34, 73, 97, 102
Frustration, 29, 75, 111, 122-124, 126, 128-130, 132-134, 151
Gentle, 36
Gentleness, 82
God, 16-19, 21, 23-25, 27-31, 33-55, 57-60, 63, 65, 67-73, 75-98, 101-102, 104-105, 115, 121-135, 137-141, 144-146, 148-149, 151
God's image, 18-19, 21, 104, 141, 143
Goodness, 29, 71, 127
Grace, 29, 41, 43, 45, 48, 78, 92, 128, 139
Grief, 90
Handicap, 11, 104, 138, 143
Handicapped, 11-12, 71
Hardship, 45, 47-48, 101, 126

Subject Index of Terms Used / 161

Harm, 26, 29, 103, 112, 118
Harmful, 78, 79
Harming, 26, 91
Heal, 29, 61, 76, 90, 138
Healing, 10, 29, 52, 55-56, 61, 65-66, 71-76, 78, 85, 87, 90-91, 133
Health, 9, 26-27, 66, 73, 112
Healthy, 8-10, 72, 91, 103, 112
Holiness, 33, 75, 78, 85-86
Holy, 46, 70-72, 75, 78, 85-100, 114, 123, 135, 149
Holy Spirit, 72, 75, 78, 85, 87-97, 114, 123, 135, 149
Hurt, 11, 29, 32, 109, 111, 129, 132, 145
Hurting, 66, 102, 105
Impairment, 8, 22-23, 25, 28, 50, 63-66, 70, 73, 76, 89, 98, 101-103, 106, 116-117, 120, 137, 141, 144, 146
Jesus, 8, 10, 23, 26, 28-29, 32-33, 37, 42, 52, 54, 56, 60-61, 65-75, 78-79, 84-87, 89-93, 96-97, 99, 101-102, 104, 107, 112, 114-115, 117, 121, 123, 128, 135-137, 141-142, 144, 147
Job, 30-31, 81-82, 122, 151
Kill, 139
Kindness, 33, 56, 82, 85
Lame, 9, 48, 55-56
Love, 7, 10, 20, 24, 37-38, 40, 55, 69, 79-82, 85, 90, 92, 101-102, 105-107, 118, 122, 126, 128-130, 133-134, 140-141
Loving, 29, 33, 38, 56, 78, 94, 102, 113, 127, 137, 139
Magnificent mammal, 13-14, 16, 18, 143
Magnificent man, 13-14, 16, 18, 21, 72, 143
Medicide, 13, 19-20
Mercy, 33, 92, 126
Moral, 10, 12, 17-20, 39, 59, 125
Morality, 20
Pain, 9-10, 29-30, 32, 39, 41, 6364, 68, 90, 111, 128, 134, 139
Painful, 30-31, 35-36, 38, 89, 90, 145
Patience, 82, 105, 121
Peace, 38-39, 81-82, 138, 140

Perseverance, 141
Perspective, 17, 20, 34, 38, 42-44, 47, 89, 101, 108, 110, 112, 124, 126, 131-132, 134, 145, 149-151
Physical impairment, 8, 28-29, 33, 35, 40-42, 45-47, 50-51, 53, 59, 63, 65, 70, 73, 76, 102, 106, 108, 116-117, 120, 135, 137-138, 140, 144-146
Physically impaired, 8-10, 12-13, 18- 24, 26, 29, 31, 48, 50, 56, 61, 64, 66, 72, 73, 89, 97-99, 100-121, 135, 140-141, 143, 146-147, 149-150
Pride, 39, 82
Prideful, 39
Punish, 33, 58, 63
Punishment, 57, 125, 139
Righteous, 66, 80, 86, 100, 132
Righteousness, 33, 38, 65 69, 70, 75, 77-78, 81-86, 96-97
Satan, 30-33, 41, 67, 81, 128
Sick, 27, 36, 61, 63, 76, 100-101, 115, 120, 150
Sickness, 36-37, 59, 66
Sin, 23-33, 36-41, 64-66, 69-71, 75-78, 90-94, 96, 112, 123, 128, 131, 139, 147
Spiritual
  growth, 115-117
  impairment, 64-66, 70, 71, 73, 76, 89, 141, 147
  maturity, 45, 75, 83, 116-118, 130
  offspring, 72, 89
  surgery, 76
  warfare, 33, 81
  victory, 72
Spiritually impaired, 66, 70, 75-76, 140, 147
Strong, 16, 26-27, 41, 47, 89, 107, 139
Strength, 24, 41, 43-44, 47-48, 55, 71, 89, 93, 121, 128, 130-131, 133, 136
Suffer, 12, 22, 27, 29, 31, 66, 72-73, 91, 102, 104, 112, 123, 140
Suffering, 20, 28, 29, 31-33, 46-48, 61, 63-69, 71, 90, 101, 123, 127, 128, 131, 137, 139, 147